WHAT NEXT

DANIEL HANNAN has been Conservative MEP for South East England since 1999. He writes frequently for the *Daily Telegraph*, *Daily Mail*, *Guardian*, *CapX*, and *Washington Examiner*. He is the author of the award-winning *How We Invented Freedom & Why It Matters* and the *Sunday Times* bestseller *Why Vote Leave*.

Also by Daniel Hannan

How We Invented Freedom & Why It Matters

Why Vote Leave

WHAT NEXT

Daniel Hannan

First published in the UK in 2016 by Head of Zeus, Ltd.

Copyright © Daniel Hannan, 2016

9 7 5 3 1 2 4 6 8

A catalogue record for this book is available from
the British Library.

ISBN (HB): 9781786691934
ISBN (E): 9781786691927

Typeset by Adrian McLaughlin

Printed and bound in Great Britain by
CPI Group (UK) Ltd, Croydon CR0 4YY

Head of Zeus Ltd
Clerkenwell House
45–47 Clerkenwell Green
London EC1R 0HT

WWW.HEADOFZEUS.COM

To Alexander Frederick Maynard Hannan,
born one month after the referendum

CONTENTS

INTRODUCTION

WILLIE WHITELAW, Margaret Thatcher's genial deputy prime minister, was fond of saying that nothing in politics is ever as good or as bad as it at first looks. It's worth reminding ourselves of that little aphorism as the vote to quit the EU turns into hard policy.

It is already obvious that things aren't as bad as was recently being claimed. During the campaign, we were repeatedly told that there would be a disastrous economic shock in the immediate aftermath of a Leave vote. The week after the referendum, a Reuters poll of City economists showed that 71 per cent were predicting a recession in 2016, a position shared by most of the main banks. Almost no one now expects that outcome, and J.P. Morgan, Goldman Sachs and the rest have quietly uprated their forecasts.

Equally, though, we shouldn't expect leaving the

EU to effect an instant and benign transformation of Britain. As I argued throughout the referendum, the day after we leave will look very much like the day before. It will be the day that we can *begin* to diverge, opting out of the costlier EU regulations, exploiting trade opportunities overseas. Brexit, I kept telling anyone who would listen, will be a process, not an event.

That process is now under way, and the attention of most commentators is on the talks in the palaces and chancelleries of Europe. The terms of our disengagement, though, are only one aspect of what happens next, and oddly not the most significant. Willie Whitelaw's dictum applies here, too. Politicians on both sides of the Channel have a perverse incentive to present the negotiations as difficult and tetchy, thereby making themselves look tough and lowering expectations before the conclusion.

In fact, there are three broad aspects to getting Brexit right: the deal we strike with our twenty-seven partners; the new relationships we form with the 165 non-EU states; and the domestic reforms we undertake in consequence. Of the three, the first is arguably the simplest, while the third is by far the most important.

No one, on either side of the Channel, is seriously calling for tariffs or other trade barriers. All sides recognize that prosperous neighbours make good customers, and that the one country's wealth raises another's. Sure, some technical aspects of the talks may drag on: the extent to which common rules apply to services; the terms on which British farmers may sell into the EU after they leave the Common Agricultural Policy; reciprocal rights to take up job offers. But these matters are, if not exactly procedural, hardly questions where our starting principles are impossibly far apart. As we shall see, it is likely that Britain will end up as the leading member of an outer circle in Europe, bringing together states that wish to trade freely with the EU but not amalgamate with it politically.

Of more importance is the issue of how we use our new global trade opportunities. Theresa May has spoken encouragingly of a post-EU Britain becoming 'the global leader in free trade', and I can't immediately think of a finer ambition. Don't make the mistake of thinking that dismantling trade barriers is essentially a dry economic process. Free trade doesn't simply put more money into the hands of the lowest earners. It doesn't just eliminate extreme poverty globally. It is also the ultimate enabler of peace, having done far more to bring countries together than any number of EU directives.

'Free trade is God's diplomacy,' said the great nineteenth-century radical MP, Richard Cobden. 'There is no other certain way of uniting people in the bonds of peace.' He was right. As Bruce Russett and John Oneal showed in their 2001 study, *Triangulating Peace*, there is no surer predictor of pacification than the opening of an economy.

Still, actually delivering free trade, in defiance of vested interests at home and abroad, and the Euro-centric assumptions of our civil servants, will not be straightforward. It will require the messianic belief of a Cobden, combined with tactical patience.

Most vital of all, though, is the third aspect: transforming our economy so as to make the most of our new opportunities while, at the same time, reforming our democracy so as to address the grievances that drove people to vote Leave.

This domestic aspect has so far had surprisingly little attention. Yet there is no purpose in leaving the EU if we simply replicate its mistakes and build our own version of Brussels corporatism. If we want to maximize our success, we need to compete. We need lower, flatter and simpler taxes; we need streamlined welfare; we need cheaper houses and cheaper energy; we need a different approach to regulation.

Some of these things will now be possible as a direct result of Brexit. Others are unrelated reforms which, in the mood of excitement and resolve which has followed the vote, are now not only politically feasible, but popular.

In the chapters to come, I shall set out ways in which these things might be done. The challenge is not to make Brexit happen: that argument has just taken place. Nor is it to make Brexit happen within a particular timescale. It seems pretty clear that Britain will leave by the end of the current European Parliament and Commission cycle in 2019: after forty-three years of membership, a few months either way make little difference.

No, the real challenge is to make the process both amicable and mutually beneficial. We must use Brexit as a way to boost our productivity and competitiveness, and to do so in a way which our European allies see as in their interests, too.

Here are fifteen broad aims that inform what follows.

1. British laws must have supremacy on our own territory. This means scrapping Articles 2 and 3 of the 1972 European Communities Act, which gives EU rulings precedence over our laws.

2. The UK should retain its free-trade arrangements with the twenty-seven EU states and the other European states and territories that have free-trade deals with the EU. At the same time, it should leave the Common External Tariff and remove duties and other barriers against imports from non-European countries.

3. Trade should be carried out, wherever possible, on the basis of mutual product recognition, rather than common standards. This principle will force a measure of deregulation on our domestic economy.

4. Britain should consider expediting its overseas trade talks by joining NAFTA and EFTA – although not the European Economic Area.

5. Taxes should be lower, simpler and flatter.

6. Welfare should be simplified and localized.

7. Government policy should not artificially raise fuel or housing costs through excessive taxation or excessive regulation.

8. Britain should remain committed to the defence of Europe, and should enlarge its commitment to NATO.

9. Britain should urgently set about dismantling tariff and non-tariff barriers with non-EU states, multilaterally whenever possible, but unilaterally if necessary.

10. Before formally triggering Article 50, we should advance our discussions on trade with non-EU states to the greatest possible extent.

11. Our preference should be for an amicable agreement with the EU that will allow for the creation of a broader European market surrounding and encompassing the remaining European Union.

12. Britain should be prepared to pay its share of any EU structures or institutions with which it is still involved; but it should not make transfer payments to other EU states simply on grounds of their level of GDP.

13. UK nationals will cease to be Citizens of the European Union, and no EU court will be able to determine who may enter or remain in the UK. Having taken back control of immigration policy, Britain should be prepared to allow EU nationals to study and work in the UK temporarily.

14. The UK should maintain the Common Travel Area within the British Isles, and impose no land border with the Irish Republic.

15. A Constitutional Convention should explore ways to devolve, disperse and decentralize powers, including the possibility of a federal structure for the UK.

After forty-three years, we have pushed the door ajar. A rectangle of light dazzles us and, as our eyes adjust, we see a summer meadow. Swallows swoop against the blue sky. We hear the gurgling of a little brook. Now to stride into the sunlight.

1

INDEPENDENCE DAY

Even now, I struggle to take in the magnitude of what happened. I can't think of a political event at once so vast and so improbable.

On 23 June, the British people politely ignored the advice of their political leaders, disregarded months of hectoring, bullying and threats and voted to leave the EU.

They did so in defiance of all the main parties; of the mega-banks and the multi-nationals; of the CBI, the TUC, the NFU and most other trade and professional associations; of the broadcasters; of domestic and international bureaucracies; and of every foreign politician from whom David Cameron or George Osborne could call in a favour.

To describe the campaign as 'David against Goliath' doesn't begin to do justice to the imbalance of forces. Had Goliath sent to Gath for reinforcements, got a gang of fifty Philistine spearmen together, rushed the shepherd boy *en masse* and still lost, it would perhaps be an adequate metaphor.

For once, the phrase 'against all the odds' is precisely apposite. On polling day, the bookmakers gave an implied probability of 18 per cent Leave, 82 per cent Remain. So it's perhaps unsurprising that, as Britain woke to the news on an appropriately sunny Friday morning, even Leave voters felt a sense of numbness, almost of shellshock.

Shall I tell you what that numbness was? It was the mildly vertiginous sense of being back in control again. It was the shock of a convalescent who, after weeks of being bed-ridden, throws open the door and strides into a sunlit garden. The shock of a paroled prisoner who, accustomed to being told when to rise, eat and exercise, suddenly has to make his own decisions.

For as long as almost anyone could remember, British voters had been accustomed to having circumscribed choices placed before them by their political elites. On 23 June 2016, they rejected all the options, and instructed their leaders to come up with a different menu.

Any doubt about the people-versus-elites nature of the vote was dispelled by the reaction of the losers. Thousands of Remain voters, mainly well-heeled Londoners, marched on Parliament, demanding that MPs ignore the result. Millions signed an online petition for a second referendum. Some corporations hired an expensive law firm, Mishcon de Reya, to attempt to stop the prime minister from initiating withdrawal proceedings without a specific vote in Parliament.

Meanwhile, a number of peers signalled that they would vote to overturn the popular decision. As Baroness Wheatcroft, a former newspaper editor, put it: 'If it comes to a bill, I think the Lords might actually delay things. There's a majority in the Lords for remaining.'[1] Tony Blair openly admitted that the tactic was to string things out for long enough to allow a general election to intervene and, as he hoped, reverse the result.[2]

What we were witnessing was the petulance of a political caste which, after years of getting its own way, found itself unexpectedly checked. I don't mean to suggest that all or even most Remain voters want a second referendum. Many of them – like many Leave voters – reached their decision narrowly, after some

1   *The Times*, 1 August 2016
2   Sky News, 3 July 2016

agonizing. And even among the more committed Remainers, polls show that most have accepted the democratic verdict equably enough.

Still, it is telling that a core of Europhile bigwigs are prepared to dismiss, not just this vote, but the whole concept of democracy. Without realizing it, they are vindicating one of the chief complaints of Leave campaigners, namely that the EU is intrinsically oligarchic, preferring technocratic rule to popular sovereignty.

Listen to some of the reactions to the vote, not just in Britain, but around the world. Here is the zoologist Richard Dawkins in the high-brow magazine, *Prospect*:

> There are stupid, ignorant people in every country but their blameless stupidity mostly doesn't matter because they are not asked to take historically momentous and irrevocable decisions of state.[3]

Here is the normally restrained American publication, *Foreign Policy*:

> It's time for the elites to rise up against the ignorant masses. Brexit has laid bare the political schism of our

3   6 July 2016

time. It's not about the left vs. the right; it's about the sane vs. the mindlessly angry.[4]

Here is the cult Slovenian philosopher, Slavoj Žižek:

Popular opinion is not always right. Sometimes I think one has to violate the will of the majority.[5]

These views, frankly, are at the politer end of the spectrum. On social media, the filters came off, and we saw what some people really thought. Several Remain campaigners reacted like spoilt toddlers, demanding that the franchise be linked to intelligence tests, raging against the elderly working-class dolts who they imagined had tipped the result, dismissing all opposition as 'bigotry' – which is deliciously ironic when we recall that the *Oxford English Dictionary* defines bigotry as 'intolerance toward those who hold different opinions to oneself'.

In their resentment of democracy, these Euro-enthusiasts were revealing a great deal about their world view. The entire process of European integration has, in a sense, been carried out at the expense of representative government. The EU was conceived

4   26 July 2016
5   'Open Democracy', 1 July 2016

as an antidote to what its founders saw as excessive democracy. Having lived through the populism and demagoguery of the 1930s, they were determined to vest supreme power in the hands of unelected officials who would be free to temper and moderate public opinion.

The trouble is that, as the years passed, Eurocrats and their auxiliaries within the member states became downright contemptuous of public opinion. As José Manuel Barroso, at that time the unelected head of the European Commission, put it in 2010:

> Governments are not always right. If governments were always right we would not have the situation that we have today. Decisions taken by the most demo-cratic institutions in the world are very often wrong.[6]

His successor, Jean-Claude Juncker, was even blunter:

> There can be no democratic choice against the Euro-pean Treaties.[7]

If you want to understand why so many people voted to withdraw, look no further than those words.

6 *Daily Telegraph*, 29 September 2010
7 *Le Figaro*, 28 January 2016 ('*Il ne peut y avoir de choix démocratique contre les traités européens.*')

The referendum result has divided Brussels into two camps. There are those who still can't bring themselves to believe that the UK will leave, who imagine that things can somehow be strung along until the British come to their senses; and there are those who are keen to amputate Britain before the Eurosceptic gangrene spreads to the Continent. There are, in other words, deniers and retrenchers. But there are no soul-searchers. No one in Brussels is asking whether Britain might have had a point. No one, at least no one I have come across, sees the Brexit vote as a reason to change direction. British voters may be dismissed as selfish bigots, or pitied as credulous fools who fell for populists; but they must on no account be taken seriously.

It's true that in some of the other twenty-seven national capitals, a different attitude prevails. Several Continental politicians recognize that their own voters share a lot of British concerns. Some are prepared to talk about using Brexit to make reforms to the EU as a whole – something which, while it is not in our gift to influence, we should none the less applaud, the success and prosperity of our immediate neighbours being of concern to us.

In the end, the views of those national politicians are likely to prove definitive. It is the twenty-seven member states, rather than the Brussels institutions, that will control the Brexit talks.

This book will explore how that process will play out. It will look at ways in which the concerns of the 48 per cent who voted Remain, as well as of the 52 per cent who voted Leave, might be accommodated in a new, looser arrangement. It will consider, not just how to make the process of disengagement cordial and mutually beneficial, but how to press home the opportunities that leaving the EU will open up. It will contemplate some of the domestic reforms that, outside the EU, are both possible and urgent.

But before I come to those things, let me reiterate a point that really shouldn't need making, but that, in the present climate, evidently does. Britain is leaving the EU. The primacy of EU law over British statutes will be terminated. Parliament will again become sovereign. Whatever arrangements we have with our friends afterwards will be based on co-operation rather than coercion, on alliance rather than assimilation, on sovereignty rather than subordination.

My sense is that most of the 48 per cent accept this fact with good grace, as do almost all the Conservative MPs who backed Remain. There are still, though, powerful and articulate irreconcilables. Tony Blair and the Europhile peers and the exquisitely suited lobbyists from the mastodon banks still dream of a second referendum, in which the UK will back down. Britain Stronger in Europe, the defeated Remain campaign, continues to send out Tweets about how frightful everything is, like some resistance movement in an occupied capital.

Yet, if they were to think about it open-mindedly, these irreconcilables would realize that a second referendum would be harder to win than the first. The polls have continued to drift toward Leave: the latest survey as I write, a YouGov poll, shows Leave ahead by 46 per cent to 42 – a far stronger position than that company registered before polling day. More to the point, the act of calling a second referendum would prompt at least some Remain voters to switch sides out of democratic principle, affronted at a political class that had refused to take no for an answer.

In any case, those hankering after a different result face a more basic problem. If you are one of those still dreaming and scheming about a second referendum, ask yourself one question: on what would you base your campaign this time? You fired off a great deal of ammunition in the run-up to 23 June, and most of it turned out to be dud. You told us that British immigration officers would be thrown out of France, and that we'd have migrant camps in Kent. In fact, within two weeks of the vote, the French government confirmed that the old arrangements would remain in place. You told us that there'd be an emergency budget. Within days of the poll, that idea was dropped.

You told us that we'd be £4,300 worse off per family, a figure that no one now tries to defend. You told us that our stock market would collapse; in fact, British stocks are, at the time of writing, the best-performing in Europe. You told us that unemployment would rise. In fact, it has fallen in the two months since the vote. You told us that there would be a recession in 2016. How's that working out?

You brought the German finance minister over to London to tell us that 'out means out', and that we'd be treated like any third country. Now that minister says that a special status will be found that protects the close commercial relationship between the UK and Germany, and that he only used that phrase at George Osborne's explicit request.

You invited Barack Obama to London to tell us that we'd be at the 'back of the queue' when it came to trade deals with the United States. Since the vote, the president has conspicuously failed to repeat that line, instead stressing the vital importance of the UK–US alliance. Meanwhile, US–EU trade talks have stalled, and Congress is instead looking at a bilateral treaty with Britain which, as the Speaker of Congress, Paul Ryan, says, will 'be easier to do' than a deal with the protectionist EU.[8]

Even Canada, which thought it had agreed its trade deal with the EU, is now drawing back, frustrated by the refusal of Romania and Bulgaria to ratify the accord unless Ottawa makes concessions in an unrelated dispute about visa-free access for Romanian and Bulgarian nationals. Indeed, at the time of writing, twenty-six states, from Australia to Uruguay, have indicated their keenness to sign commercial accords with a post-EU Britain, recognizing that such a Britain will be more liberal than the EU.

Meanwhile, the IMF, whose dire prophecies of woe and destruction were the mainstay of the Remain campaign, has been lacerated by its own watchdog, which accuses it of being so *in hoc* to the euro project that it forgot its purpose. I had opposed Christine Lagarde's appointment to the IMF on precisely these grounds: I argued at the time that she had an obsession with European integration that would override other considerations. When she made her repeated interventions in the UK referendum at George Osborne's request, I and other Leave campaigners tried to point out that she was hardly impartial, but we

8 WBEL, 24 June 2016

were told to listen to the experts. Then, a month after the vote, the IMF's Independent Evaluation Office complained of the 'groupthink' that had promoted 'the view supportive of what was perceived to be Europe's political project', and which prejudiced what ought to have been the IMF's core function.

If people didn't listen to these supposedly expert warnings last time, they certainly won't do so now, when those warnings have been shown to be wrong.

The question, in short, is not whether we leave the EU, or even when we leave the EU, since it seems pretty clear that the moment of formal departure will be at some point in 2019. The question, rather, is how to leave amicably and on terms that are beneficial to both sides.

A persistent Remain complaint, both during the campaign and, even more so, since the vote, is that Leave campaigners 'have no plan'. In fact, Vote Leave had a doorstopper of a plan: a million-word study called *Change or Go*, which looked at everything from tariff schedules to fisheries rights. That document, which was widely recognized as both detailed and authoritative, set out the kind of renegotiation that Britain should pursue as an existing member. Plainly, things have now moved on, but the substance of the paper still applies. There is a comprehensive scheme, showing how, within the broad nexus of a European free market, Britain can recover sovereignty, restore her trading links with non-EU states and exploit the competitive advantages that will come with independence.

The issue before us is, in effect, how much of that plan to implement. We can't disregard the fact that 48 per cent of Britons voted for the status quo. We need to listen to their concerns, both on economic matters and on the other priorities they raised during the campaign, such as continued participation in various EU educational and research programmes. It may well be that, when we leave the EU, we choose to replicate through bilateral deals some of the arrangements that we are currently locked into as members.

Nor can we ignore the fact that the UK is a partnership of four nations, and that two of those – Scotland and Northern Ireland – returned pro-EU majorities. We should look for a new status that all the home nations can live with – a relationship with the EU which may be too close for some and too distant for others, but that majorities in all four constituent parts of the realm can at least accept.

Think back to the referendum on Scottish independence in September 2014. That result, too, was narrow, with 45 per cent of Scots voting for complete separation and 55 per cent voting for the status quo. After such an outcome, all sides quickly recognized that the only way to build a new consensus in Scotland would be with something in between those two positions – a new dispensation, with more devolution, including fiscal autonomy, stopping short of full independence.

There is no dishonour in seeking a similar compromise now. Those of us who believe in democracy must accept it in spirit as well as in letter. We have a mandate to leave the EU, but it is not a mandate to sever all links. A post-EU Britain will not simply relate to the EU as a benign third country in the way that, say, Japan does. Just as Remain voters must accept that Britain voted to quit the EU, so Leave voters must accept that it did so only marginally. Interpreting a 52–48 result will mean leaving the EU, but retaining some institutional links with it.

This book will set out how to secure such a deal with maximum advantage to the United Kingdom and to the rest of the EU. Before we turn to that process, though, let us look at how we came to this point. We need the fullest sense of what the country voted for before we seek to turn that result into hard policy.

Since the referendum, a lot of journalists who backed Remain have become overnight experts on what Leavers 'really' wanted. As someone who spent his entire adult life campaigning against the EU, I can perhaps offer a better close-up view of what happened than some of those pundits. The story is worth telling from the start. Only when we have coldly considered what people voted for and why, should we turn to how to implement their instructions.

2

THE LONG MARCH

WHEN I was nineteen, I swore what the old adventure stories call 'a terrible oath' to restore Britain's independence. It was 1991, and I was in my first year as an undergraduate at Oxford. Margaret Thatcher had recently been turfed out of office by a coalition of EU leaders and Euro-integrationist Tory backbenchers, both frustrated by her hostility to monetary union.

In retrospect, it seems extraordinary that Britain's most successful post-war prime minister could have been toppled over an issue on which, as almost everyone now accepts, she was right. It's true that Mrs Thatcher was already in a weak position domestically, with unrest over the poll tax and unhappiness about her style of government. Still, even as a teenager watching the drama of politics for the first time, I marvelled at the power of the Brussels establishment.

Picking up the phrase from an adult novel by C. S. Lewis that I was reading at the time, I thought of it as the European machine's 'hideous strength'. It was a phrase that I was to find useful over the next quarter of a century. Again and again, national leaders were forced to act against their personal, party and national interests for the sake of closer integration.

Heads of government could be ousted, as Mrs Thatcher had been, when they became inconvenient. Bertie Ahern was forced to stand aside so as not to endanger Ireland's ratification of the Lisbon treaty; George Papandreou and Silvio Berlusconi were removed in civilian putsches – all because they stood in the way of the European project.

The coup against Mrs Thatcher turned out to be, from a Euro-integrationist point of view, a roaring success. Within a few months of taking over as prime minister, John Major was on his way to the pretty Dutch border town of Maastricht to put his name to the first draft of the eponymous treaty.

Maastricht marked the moment at which the European Economic Community ceased to be a club of nations focused chiefly on commercial matters, and became instead a political union. It extended

Brussels' jurisdiction into a series of non-economic fields: criminal justice, social policy, employment law, defence, foreign affairs, culture, media, immigration, citizenship rights. It committed most of the member states to merge their national currencies.

Just in case anyone missed the point, the change in the scope and functions of the European institutions was reflected in a new name. The European Economic Community (and its sister organizations, the European Coal and Steel Community and the European Atomic Energy Community) became the European Union. Eurocrats bestowed on that Union many of the attributes and trappings of nationhood: a flag, a national anthem, a national day, a common passport and driving licence, shared embassies.

No one in Brussels denied that the goal was to turn the EU into a single state. As the sign in the European Commission building put it: 'Europe – Your Country'. The man running that Commission, Jacques Delors, would unfold his plan to anyone who listened. He wanted the European Commission to become the cabinet of the new federal state, while the European Parliament became its legislature and the Council of Ministers became a sort of Senate or *Bundesrat* representing the provinces – that is, the member states. It was these three specific proposals that had prompted Margaret Thatcher's famous response: 'No! No! No!'

It is worth noting, by the way, that none of these aims has been retracted. On the contrary, federation remains the formal stated goal of the European Commission and, for that matter, of the leaders of the main member states. 'Of course the European Commission will one day become a government, the EU council a second chamber and the European Parliament will have more powers,' says Angela Merkel, the German chancellor.[9]

'For my children's future I dream, think and work for the United States of Europe,' says the Italian premier, Matteo Renzi.[10]

'What threatens us is not too much Europe, but a lack of it,' agrees the French president, François Hollande.[11]

Such views have been mainstream since the Maastricht Treaty. Although there had been premonitions and hints in earlier documents, they had, until 1992, been rhetorical rather than institutional. Maastricht gave the federalist vision structural form. More than that, it gave it orthodoxy. A federal Europe

9   *EUobserver*, 7 November 2012
10 Speech in Florence, 9 May 2014
11 *Journal du Dimanche*, 18 July 2015

was no longer just one among a series of competing ideas; it was now official policy.

It is already becoming hard to recall the convulsions in British politics prompted by this shift. Until the 1990s, 'Europe' was debated largely as an economic proposition. Most MPs, in most parties, backed membership on commercial grounds, without giving much thought to what the French called the *finalité politique* – that is, the goal of eventual fusion. To the extent that they were aware of European federalism, they tended to dismiss it as the sort of overblown waffle to which excitable Continentals, though splendid fellows in their way, were regrettably prone.

Maastricht forced those MPs to confront the truth. It became impossible to discuss the EU without at least allowing that the eventual aim was political amalgamation. John Major's government briefly tried to present its support for the Maastricht Treaty as a tactical and reluctant necessity; but that strategy collapsed when, on 2 June 1992, Denmark rejected the treaty in a referendum. Instead of following through the logic of his previous position and dropping ratification, John Major connived at a scheme to force Maastricht on the Danes in a second vote. He and his ministers now took to arguing openly for political union as a desirable end in itself.

In those days, British politicians had not realized how unpopular such talk was. They had not learned to curb their tongues, to keep quiet and let the EU institutions do the work of deeper integration. Instead (to their credit, in a way), they argued openly for political union as the way to have power in the world – the way to stand up to China and Japan and Russia and America.

Paddy Ashdown, the Liberal Democrat leader, kept repeating a joke about how he was 'not afraid to use the f-word – "federalism"'. The leader of Labour's MEPs, David Martin, proudly declared: 'Let's stop defending, pretending and apologizing. A socialist superstate is precisely what we want to create.'[12] MPs in all parties tended to see the euro as a matter of when rather than if. Throughout the Major years, no Conservative could sit as a frontbencher while expressing the view that joining the single currency was wrong in principle.

For the country at large, the idea of merger into a European federation came without warning, like a sudden rain shower on a sunny day. One moment, we were in a club of nations; the next, we were being told that the very notion of nationhood was redundant, and that a United States of Europe was a historical

12 'Europe: An Ever-Closer Union', 1991

necessity. All sorts of ideas, from the euro to the setting of common social standards and labour rules, went from being unthinkable to being inevitable without any intervening stage.

For me, at nineteen, the crystallizing moment came during a visit by the Latvian foreign minister to London. The USSR had recently broken apart, and some of its constituent members were moving faster than others toward establishing the institutions of statehood. Asked whether his country was now truly sovereign, he replied artlessly: 'Latvia is now more independent than the United Kingdom.'

It was true. Indeed, as a matter of legal fact, it was incontrovertible. Britain, which had fought two monstrous wars to protect the sovereignty of friendly countries, and thereby ensured that democracies around Europe could retain their independence, was less independent than the newborn Baltic republic.

I decided there and then that recovering our self-government was the most important issue in politics. At a meeting in the Queen's Lane Coffee House, I set up the Oxford Campaign for an Independent Britain, dedicated to ending the supremacy of European over British law. There were two other students at that first meeting: Mark Reckless, who went on to become a Conservative MP before dramatically crossing the floor to UKIP; and James Ross, now an internationally active conductor. We quickly realized that we had tapped into a growing mood. By the end of its first term, the Oxford CIB had more than 300 members. Within a year, branches were springing up in other universities.

In the early 1990s, it seemed natural for students to be both anti-Establishment and anti-EU. We could see bankers, bureaucrats and politicians backing a project that worked for them, rather than for the general population. We'd have been astonished to learn that, a generation later, students would be lining up alongside Shell and Unilever and Goldman Sachs, cheering on the Eurocrats who toured Europe in private jets to preach austerity. The change in the attitudes of young people generally, and students especially, has come about only very recently, for reasons we shall come to presently.

Back in the early 1990s, though, we could sense that we were at the start of something. Britain was stirring: we felt it in our bones. The Oxford CIB was one of many organizations that had either been called into being or resuscitated by Maastricht. There were new associations, like the Bruges Group and Conservatives Against a Federal Europe. There were established ones like the Freedom Association that now made Euroscepticism their priority. And there were organizations that had been in near-hibernation since the 1975 referendum, such as the Labour Euro Safeguards Campaign, which now roused themselves, shook off their slumber and ambled into the watery light.

Euroscepticism had been largely extinguished in 1975, when the country voted by two to one to remain in the EEC. The last embers were stamped out when Michel Foot's anti-EEC Labour Party was crushed in 1983. After that, the issue disappeared from the public arena. A handful of brave MPs did their best to stir the cinders back into flame: Richard Shepherd, John Biffen, Teddy Taylor, Richard Body and Jonathan Aitken on the Conservative side; Peter Shore, Tony Benn, Bob Cryer, Austin Mitchell, Eric Deakins and David Stoddart for Labour. Enoch Powell would occasionally descend from the hills, like an Old Testament prophet, to call the people to righteousness. But even he, the finest orator of his age, struggled to interest voters in a subject that everyone thought closed.

Then, in the early 1990s, it began to dawn on people that the prophecies they had dismissed as utterly improbable – the jeremiads about superstates and single currencies and common taxation – were coming true. Almost overnight, those extinct cinders burst into bright orange flame.

Between 1992 and 2016, the European question never went away. Sometimes, a conflagration would roar, as when the government held on by one or two parliamentary votes during the passage of Maastricht; sometimes the flames would flicker more dimly; but they were never again extinguished. Each subsequent European treaty – Amsterdam, Nice, Lisbon – pushed more powers from the national capitals to Brussels. And each one provoked stronger resistance in Britain – and, latterly, in other EU states, too.

I spent those years waging a long, gruelling, unsuccessful guerrilla campaign against the project. I spent part of one university summer in Bill Cash's constituency home in Staffordshire, drafting the thousands of amendments that were to slow the passage of the Maastricht Bill. Bill was at that time leading the chief Eurosceptic group, known as the European Foundation. My co-drafter was a postgraduate student from London called Syed Kamall, who went on to become my boss in the European Parliament as leader of the European Conservatives and Reformists.

I organized a protest in Bath when the EU finance ministers held their summit there in September 1992, bringing several of my Oxford CIB friends over to demonstrate against the disastrous ERM. Images of our protest filled Europe's TV screens all weekend and, by the following Wednesday, Britain was blessedly out of the system.

The following month, I was gathering signatures at the Conservative Party Conference in Brighton in support of the group of MPs who went on to try to prevent Maastricht being ratified, the Fresh Start Group.

Maastricht became law shortly before I took my finals in 1993, and I went on to work for a group of Eurosceptic Conservative MPs, half of whom had been rebels and half reluctant loyalists, chaired by the clever and amiable Michael Spicer. We worked to put together a network of anti-federalist parliamentarians from all over Europe, several of whom went on, years afterwards, to become Tory allies in the European Parliament.

Meeting under the deliberately innocuous name of European Research Group, we set out the changes the EU would need to make to restore democracy to its component nations. We worked with economists and businessmen to show what was wrong with the single currency, and why Britain should stay out. We brought in legal experts to propose ways in which national constitutions could again be made supreme over the European Court of Justice (ECJ), whose primacy had been established, not in a treaty, but by a judicial coup d'état.

At the same time, we brought together several Eurosceptic groups, including some at the more bloody-minded end of the spectrum, under an umbrella organization called the Congress for Democracy. Michael Spicer's deceptively understated and agreeable manner in the chair allowed many different groups to co-operate, including business leaders and trade union shop stewards, as well as activists from UKIP and the Referendum Party.

We were winning the battle of ideas; but we were losing the battle of implementation. As the public debate went on, it became less and less acceptable for politicians to admit to supporting federalism. Yet jurisdiction continued to shift, day after day, from Westminster to Brussels.

It was easy for Eurosceptics to become downhearted. I was almost a full-time campaigner against deeper union throughout those years, first as a newspaper columnist and then as an MEP; and I sometimes felt, with Tolkien's Galadriel, that I was 'fighting the long defeat'. Each time some new power was handed to the EU – the European Arrest Warrant, say, or the creation of EU embassies – I would inveigh against it. Opinion polls suggested that what I was saying was popular: people wanted substantial powers back from the EU. Yet the same polls indicated a certain weariness, a sense that the powers that be would never listen.

I travelled across Europe in the anti-federalist cause. I campaigned in referendums in France, Denmark (several times), Sweden, Spain and the Netherlands. More often than not, we Eurosceptics won the vote. But it never seemed to make any difference.

You could hardly blame people for becoming cynical. But I remembered something that Enoch Powell had said after the 1975 referendum result. Asked whether his life's work was now in ruins, he told the interviewer that, as a young man in the 1930s, he had expected an unprepared and idle Britain to be defeated in the war with Germany that he could see coming. 'At the beginning of my life,' he said, 'I made the mistake of despairing of my countrymen. I shall not repeat that mistake at the end of my life.'

In any case, the gradual change in the temper of the Conservative Party gave rational grounds for optimism. Each new intake of MPs was more Eurosceptic than the last. In 1997, a Eurosceptic Tory MP was one who opposed the single currency; almost no one seriously questioned Britain's membership of the EU. By 2010, a Eurosceptic Tory MP was one who wanted to leave the EU; almost no one seriously proposed joining the euro.

Those new MPs, it struck me, were reflecting public opinion. The system was working. The distance between Brussels and the nations – or, to be precise, between the political classes and everyone else – could not keep widening for ever, even in an imperfect democracy. Sooner or later, one of the main parties would have to turn and swim with the current.

It is worth stressing that the common demand of almost all the Eurosceptic groups at this time, on Left and Right, was a recovery of sovereignty – or, to put it in less abstract terms, a recovery of the right to decide our own affairs. Many, indeed, would have been satisfied with a pre-Maastricht arrangement, whereby competence was conceded only in strictly delineated economic matters. Immigration was an issue only to the extent that it was one of the many areas where we sought a recovery of Westminster jurisdiction.

Large-scale immigration from the Continent began after 2004, when ten new countries with significantly lower wage levels joined the EU. Tony Blair had announced in advance that, unlike twelve of the other then fourteen existing states, Britain would not apply transitional controls to inward migration from these ten new members.

At first, he received only mild reproaches – and such criticism as there was came largely from the Left. It became fashionable for *Guardian* writers, in particular, to complain that Blair was using EU enlargement as a way to reduce settlement from Commonwealth countries, and so – in the phrase of the time – to 'whiten up' immigration into Britain.

But it soon became clear that the PM had got the numbers wrong – so colossally wrong that it must rank as one of the greatest miscalculations of modern British politics. The Labour government's official estimate, commissioned by the Home Office, had been that between 5,000 and 13,000 migrants would enter the UK each year. In the event, 447,000 had arrived within the first two years, and more than a million were to follow.

So vast was the discrepancy between the politicians' discourse and the reality that, in the circumstances, the public response was surprisingly restrained. Most people reacted with disappointment rather than rage, concluding that the politicians who had made that promise were either congenital liars or hopeless idiots. Either way, they could see that EU membership had made a nonsense of what their leaders had promised them.

Their sense of disdain deepened when the incoming Conservative government promised to bring immigration down to below 100,000 a year, only to find that every reduction in the number of arrivals from outside the EU was swallowed up by increases in numbers from Europe. It was clear that the Tories' manifesto pledge could not be met while Britain remained in the EU; yet ministers preferred to face down the electorate rather than face down Brussels.

It would have been bizarre had a fiasco on this scale not prompted a public reaction. Some commentators were and still are determined to attribute Euroscepticism to anti-immigrant or anti-foreigner sentiment, but the backlash had a far more obvious cause. People could see that their politicians had made a solemn promise but that, when that promise clashed with the requirements of EU membership, they had abandoned it rather than challenge the EU. It was a vivid confirmation of their belief that how they voted didn't much matter as long as Brussels had ultimate power.

The suspicion that allegiance to the EU trumped both honesty and democracy deepened when David Cameron dropped his pledge to hold a referendum on the Lisbon Treaty. That pledge was not just one among many commitments offered by the opposition party. It was phrased in deliberately unequivocal language, and presented – this seems extraordinary in retrospect – as an answer to the lack of confidence in politicians' promises. David Cameron offered his 'cast-iron guarantee' in an article in the *Sun* in September 2007, which is worth quoting at length:

> The final reason we must have a vote is trust. Gordon Brown talks about 'new' politics. But there's nothing 'new' about breaking your promises to the British public. It's classic Labour. And it is the cancer that is eating away at trust in politics. Small wonder that so many people don't believe a word politicians ever say if they break their promises so casually. If you really want to signal you're a break from the past, Prime Minister, do the right thing – give the people the referendum you promised.
>
> Today, I will give this cast-iron guarantee: if I become PM a Conservative government will hold a referendum on any EU treaty that emerges from these negotiations. No treaty should be ratified without consulting the British people in a referendum.

When a politician writes in such terms, he expects people to believe him. And, indeed, that pledge marked a turning point in the fortunes of the Tory opposition. Having languished in the low thirties in the opinion polls since Gordon Brown became prime minister, the party almost immediately rose to around 40 per cent, partly because of the referendum pledge, and partly because of its simultaneous promise to reduce inheritance tax.

Other than during a brief dip when the Westminster expenses crisis hit, the Tories remained close to or above 40 per cent in the polls for the next two years. It began to look as if a promise made in the depths of opposition, when no one expected a Conservative government, might actually have to be implemented. Not for the first time, the prospect of office led to an evaporation of Euroscepticism.

David Cameron must have known that retreating from the pledge he had made in such forceful language would do him immense damage. Even voters who couldn't care less about the EU would react badly to so flagrant a climbdown. And yet, in another demonstration of the EU's hideous strength, he decided that breaking his word was preferable to taking on Brussels. On 4 November 2009, David Cameron announced that the pledge was no longer operative.

That decision probably cost him a parliamentary majority the following May. Until his U-turn, David

Cameron had seemed a remarkably fresh and honest party leader, especially in contrast to the tortured Gordon Brown. Overnight, he became, in many people's eyes, just another smooth-talking politician. The polls promptly fell back and, when the election came, no party had a majority.

The abandonment of the 'cast-iron guarantee' was the defining moment of David Cameron's years as opposition leader. I was especially disappointed, having always liked the man, and having backed him enthusiastically as party leader – a choice which I have never regretted because, setting aside our differences on the EU, I regard him as a remarkably successful prime minister, who brought our country back from the brink of financial ruin.

I never felt let down by David Cameron's support for the EU, because I had never had any illusions about it. On the contrary, I had always thought it to his credit that, unlike many front-line Tories of that era, he never pretended to be secretly more Eurosceptic than he could publicly admit. Still, I couldn't understand how a commitment made in such flinty language – a commitment explicitly offered as a way to restore people's trust in politicians – could be tossed aside.

I resigned my admittedly somewhat paltry front-bench position in the European Parliament in protest and, before announcing my decision, thought it courteous to inform the PM's office. Downing Street, of course, saw the whole thing in terms of short-term media management, and a senior aide to David Cameron called to ask me what journalists I was talking to. I replied that, if it would make him happy, I wouldn't talk to any journalists at all, but I wanted him to understand that he had just lost his last opportunity to hold a referendum on something other than membership of the EU. After such a climbdown, I told him, nothing less than an In–Out poll would do, and I thought it only polite to let him know that I intended now to campaign full-time to get such a poll. The aide chuckled indulgently and said, 'Well, good luck with that.'

I wasn't alone in realizing that the issue had now moved on to withdrawal. The breaking of the 'cast-iron guarantee' solidified an impression that had long been forming in people's minds – a sense that, as well as being undemocratic in itself, the EU served to corrode our domestic democracy. UKIP began to rise in the polls; and, in the Conservative Party, for the first time since Maastricht had passed its Third Reading, a large group of MPs began to organize themselves around opposition to the EU.

As I had promised the PM's adviser, I promptly set

about putting together a campaign to secure an In–Out referendum. The obvious vehicle was the Democracy Movement, which was a sort of lineal successor to Jimmy Goldsmith's Referendum Party. It had a large database of supporters and, more important, it had studiously avoided being pigeonholed as Left or Right, making its arguments on narrowly democratic grounds. It was run at that time by Stuart Coster and Marc Glendening – a brilliant café intellectual who had somehow, I'm glad to say, wandered into political activism. We decided to set up a group that would push exclusively for a referendum, without taking any position on what the outcome of that referendum should be.

We settled on the name 'People's Pledge', and were careful to avoid the more familiar Eurosceptic faces at our launch. Prominent among our early supporters were Labour's Natascha Engel and Keith Vaz. Within five days, we had 42,000 registered supporters and 3,000 volunteers. The press reaction was overwhelmingly positive. Trevor Kavanagh, grand old man of the Commons lobby, called us 'the first serious, credible and accelerating campaign for a proper referendum since 1975'.[13] He was right.

Our first director was Mark Seddon, a former

13 *The Sun*, 21 March 2011

editor of *Tribune* who, rather to the horror of his party's establishment, had been elected to Labour's National Executive Committee. He was succeeded by Ian McKenzie, an old-fashioned Labour Rightist and trade-union man who favoured EU membership but strongly supported a referendum. The day-to-day support came from John Mills, Labour's largest private donor, and Patrick Barbour, a quietly patriotic businessman. I set about drumming up support in the press, and Daniel Hodson, a genial former chief executive of LIFFE, started raising the money we'd need. It was the beginning of Daniel's heroic (though largely unreported) contribution to securing the eventual Leave vote. I've never known a more seductive fundraiser.

The People's Pledge was the most effective popular campaign I have ever been involved with, and must be reckoned one of the most successful pressure groups in British history. It launched in March 2011, with the stated aim of persuading at least one of the big parties to commit to holding a referendum on EU membership. At the time, that goal was dismissed on all sides with, so to speak, the same indulgent chuckle that I had had from David Cameron's aide. Yet, within twenty-two months, an In–Out referendum was Conservative policy.

How did we do it? By sticking to a very simple strategy: we invited people, in every constituency, to sign a pledge saying that at the next election they would vote only for a candidate who had promised to support a referendum on EU membership. We knew that if enough people signed our pledge, MPs would elbow each other aside to follow.

Of course, several MPs, in all parties, already backed a referendum, including some decent and democracy-minded Labour Europhiles. The challenge was to expand their number, so that being pro-referendum became an unremarkable position. We knew that once enough MPs signed up, we would reach a critical mass. If backing a referendum became sufficiently widespread, there would come a point when rational self-interest pushed MPs toward backing us. It was a classic example of tipping-point theory.

How to expedite that process? The simplest way was to start holding unofficial referendums in marginal seats. We would fund a complete postal ballot of every registered voter in a constituency, leaving the administration of the election to the Electoral Reform Society, which specializes in running ballots.

Before selecting each constituency, we would announce a shortlist of marginal seats, knowing that the MPs representing them would be horrified by the idea of finding themselves at odds with a large chunk of their electorate.

It worked. Our first constituency-wide poll, held in April 2012, was in Thurrock, a marginal Tory seat in Essex. Unsurprisingly, people overwhelmingly backed a referendum: 89.9 per cent of voters said they wanted an official In–Out poll. The key figure, though, was the participation rate. Would local voters turn out in sufficient numbers to spook anti-referendum MPs?

In the event, the turnout was 30.4 per cent, higher than at most local and European elections, and above that at Thurrock's previous council election – an extraordinary result given the non-binding nature of the ballot. Pressing home our advantage, we announced that we were going to roll out similar ballots, constituency by constituency, across the UK. First, in order to demonstrate that we had not had an atypical result in Eurosceptic Essex, we'd ballot two seats in Manchester with white-collar, public sector, Lib Dem electorates. Then we'd ballot ten more constituencies throughout the country. Then a hundred.

'How the hell are we going to afford a hundred?' I asked our director. The Electoral Reform Society, having a semi-monopolistic position when it comes to carrying out independent ballots, is not cheap. I wondered whether even Daniel Hodson would be able to elicit the necessary moolah. 'Oh, it'll never come to the hundred,' replied Ian McKenzie cheerfully. 'One or both big parties will fold long before then.'

He was spot on. After the two Manchester results, Cheadle and Hazel Grove, which saw turnouts of 35 per cent, MPs flocked to sign up. A critical moment came in October 2012, when the Conservative MPs David Nuttall and John Baron, assisted by my old friend from the Queen's Lane Coffee House, Mark Reckless, managed to secure 111 Commons votes for an In–Out referendum, despite the formal opposition of all three front benches. Two government aides, Adam Holloway and Stewart Jackson, resigned so as to, as they put it, keep faith with their constituents and restore a sense of honour to the Commons. Watching that debate, I knew that we were near the tipping point.

Almost as important as the balance in Parliament was the early support of Boris Johnson. It is worth stressing that Boris signed the pledge long before it was fashionable to do so, and his backing added to the sense of inevitability. As the political columnist James Forsyth wrote shortly afterwards:

> The Romford Pledge might not have the same ring to it
> as the Tamworth Manifesto. But Boris Johnson's deci-
> sion while campaigning last month to sign up to the
> campaign for an in/out referendum on EU membership
> could be a key moment in the history of the Conser-
> vative Party – the moment when the party's balance
> of power tipped decisively in favour of a referendum.[14]

James was right. Although it was not until the following
January that David Cameron announced his U-turn,
I could also feel the see-saw tilting, and my focus started
to shift from securing the referendum to winning it.
I knew how powerful the forces ranged against us
would be. I knew the awesome psychological power of
the status quo. To triumph, we would need the finest
campaign in modern British history. And I knew just
the man to run it.

May 2011 had seen the second of the UK's three
nationwide referendums (the first and third were both
on leaving the EU, in 1975 and 2016 respectively).
The question was whether to replace the existing electoral system, First Past the Post, with the Alternative
Vote (AV). When the AV referendum was announced
after the 2010 general election, opinion polls indicated

14 'Why a European Referendum is now almost certain', *Spectator*,
   12 May 2012

a two-to-one majority in favour of the change, and supporters of electoral reform were confident. After all, they enjoyed the backing of every political party except the Tories (who were at that stage equivocal) and Northern Ireland's Unionists (who were opposed). They had a significant financial advantage, thanks to large donations from the Joseph Rowntree Trust and the Electoral Reform Society. They were cheered on by most celebrities and public figures. And they had a cadre of activists who had been waiting all their adult lives for this moment.

Yet, when the polls closed a year later, the public had turned 180 degrees. A two-to-one lead for AV had been transformed into a two-to-one victory for First Past the Post.

Many people were responsible for that result, but one in particular stood out: Matthew Elliott, who had been seconded from the TaxPayers' Alliance to run NOtoAV, the official campaign group on the No side.

The results spoke for themselves. To flip public opinion when all the energy was on the other side showed great tactical skill. But what really impressed me was the character that Matthew had displayed during the campaign.

I sometimes think you need to have been in politics to understand how much more devastating friendly fire is than ordnance hurled at you from the other side. Politicians deal in exaggeration and calumny. In a campaign, you expect vast amounts of ammunition to be loosed at you by the opposition. It barely registers. Criticism from your own side is another matter: it can be personally wounding as well as politically damaging.

During the AV referendum, plenty of opponents of change opened up at Matthew with all guns. He was, they wrote, throwing away the campaign because of his misconceived strategy. Instead of focusing on the big, constitutional issues, he kept banging on about something utterly trivial, namely the cost of the referendum and of any subsequent change.

In the eyes of many anti-AV columnists and MPs, this was an idiotic argument. Who cared about spending a few million pounds when the total UK budget was over £700 billion? In any case, most of that money was going on the referendum itself; it couldn't be recouped by voting No.

Yet Matthew had the strength of personality to disregard all the criticism and stick to what the polling numbers were telling him. When the results were declared, I decided on the spot that he was the man to do something similar when we eventually secured our In–Out vote.

By the summer of 2012, I was convinced that such a poll was coming and, in the beautiful garden of a Norfolk holiday home where we were staying as guests of Rodney Leach and Jessica Douglas-Home, I asked Matthew if he'd be prepared to take the task on. It was no small request. Matthew knew as well as I did how one-sided the eventual campaign would be. But he also realized that this was going to be our only shot at restoring our independence. If the referendum resulted in a vote to stay in, Eurocrats would see it as the removal of the chief obstacle in the path of the superstate. The 'British problem', as they saw it, would be solved. The federalist scheme would have a renewed democratic mandate.

Neither Matthew nor I could be confident of victory; but, as we talked, I could see that he was thinking, not as a strategist, but as a patriot. The task of running the anti-EU campaign would mean taking on a short-term job, without much certainty of income, and with few prospects of success. Losing would damage his future employability. But none of that mattered. In an emergency, you drop what you're doing and rush to play your part. I could tell that Matthew was looking at the offer, not as an opportunity, but as a duty. By the time we left the flatlands of Norfolk, he was on board.

Shortly afterwards, we took the first step, establishing Business for Britain. Our idea was to set up a number of sectoral interest groups, each speaking to their own constituency: Farmers for Britain, Sikhs for Britain, Students for Britain and so on. But we were in no doubt that we had to start with our leading industrialists and financiers.

In part, this was for a practical reason. We knew that we would need a lot of money and that, while Vapers for Britain or Historians for Britain might be able to fund themselves, they would not generate a surplus. But the bigger reason was a strategic one. We were determined not to concede the economic argument.

We knew that if the campaign came down to 'less immigration versus more prosperity', people would grumble about the immigration but vote for the prosperity. If one side was talking about trade and investment while the other was talking about Romanians and Bulgarians, the first side would sound more grown up.

So it was vital, right from the start, to put in place a network of business leaders, locally as well as nationally, who could make the economic case for leaving. Between April 2013 and October 2015, when Vote Leave was formed, Business for Britain was the main vehicle for the Eurosceptic campaign. Without the support of the entrepreneurs who stepped forward at that time – Peter Cruddas, Neville Baxter, Alan Halsall, Luke Johnson, Jon Moynihan, Patrick Barbour, John Hoerner, Brian Kingham, Robert Hiscox, John Mills, Adrian McAlpine – the campaign would never have made it off the runway.

Unlike some of the business leaders who backed the other side, none of these men was hoping for a gong, a favourable contract from the government or any other gain. Some, indeed, were aware that they were forfeiting honours that might otherwise have come their way. Like everyone who contributed to or campaigned for Vote Leave, they were doing what they believed to be right for their country without hope of personal reward.

While that could also be said of many sincere rank-and-file Remainers, it was evidently not true of all of the grandees who contributed to that campaign. Plenty of Remain campaigners were decorated in David Cameron's resignation honours; and, as a rule in politics, for every honour actually awarded, a dozen are hoped for or hinted at.

The greatest contribution made by the Eurosceptic business leaders was political rather than financial. They were able to make the case, in the pages of the *FT*, in local chambers of commerce, in board-rooms and on the airwaves for a global, free-trading Britain. They made it impossible for the Remain side to portray Leave as nativist or protectionist.

Since the vote, there has been a concerted attempt to rewrite the history of British Euroscepticism: to paint it as anti-modern, anti-market, anti-immigrant or anti-foreigner. In reality – and I have been as involved as any other human being with the campaign over the past quarter of a century – it was always chiefly about democracy. Immigration featured as one of many areas where we wanted to take back control, along with taxation, criminal justice, fisheries and the rest.

Ah, you say, but what about the campaign itself? What about Nigel Farage's 'Breaking Point' poster? Can I deny that we were carried across the line by popular hostility to immigration?

As a matter of fact, I was in the Vote Leave office when that poster was unveiled and, all around me, staffers were burying their heads in their hands and groaning. They knew that that sort of message could only hurt Leave's prospects.

And sure enough, when a team of LSE academics reverse-engineered the state of public opinion – that is, went back over the polls in the light of the actual result to show how opinion had really moved throughout the campaign – they found that the day that poster was launched saw the biggest swing to Remain of the entire campaign.[15]

That swing may, of course, have been influenced by other factors, such as the abominable murder of Jo Cox, a popular Labour MP, later that day. It may simply have reflected the drift back to the status quo that many referendums see in the final week. There was no question, though, that that poster was a net negative.

How could it have been otherwise? It is impossible – literally impossible – to imagine an undecided voter seeing it and saying to himself: 'There's a migration crisis on the Continent? I didn't know that! I'd better vote Leave!'

The 'Breaking Point' poster was the last in a series of unhelpful interventions by Nigel Farage and his accomplice Arron Banks. Again and again, they seemed desperate to grab the limelight, whatever the damage to the campaign. After repeated attempts to reason with them, we were forced to the conclusion that they were less interested in winning than in using the referendum as a vehicle to promote UKIP in general and Nigel in particular.

15 Harold D. Clarke, Matthew Goodwin and Paul Whiteley, LSE, 5 July 2016

I realize that that is a big claim. But it is hard to see how else to explain the behaviour of Banks and his outfit, Leave.EU. Look back at their press releases, Tweets and interviews. They don't seem especially interested in knocking the EU; their constant focus, rather, is on assaulting the main Leave campaign. There were frequent and vicious attacks on Nigel Lawson, Matthew Elliott, Douglas Carswell and Suzanne Evans; but relatively few on the Brussels institutions.

As Banks himself admitted in an interview: 'The enemy for us is not the "in" campaign – they're laughable – the enemy is our own side. Our job is to defeat the enemy and move on.'[16] And, although he failed to defeat that enemy, every staffer who worked for Vote Leave will tell you that Banks and Leave.EU did more harm to the Eurosceptic cause than did anyone on the Remain side.

Behavioural psychologists teach us to infer motive from action. During the campaign, Banks sent lawyers' letters threatening Vote Leave board members; he sent a bizarre email hinting that they were being trailed by private detectives; he even gave out the emails and phone numbers of key Vote Leave staff, just weeks before polling day, and encouraged people to spam

16 *The Times*, 6 February 2016

them. Does that strike you as the behaviour of someone who wanted to win?

His attitude stood in marked contrast to that of the UKIP rank and file, who had been waiting a long time for their moment, and who threw themselves cheerfully and energetically into the campaign. I travelled the length of the UK during the first half of 2016, campaigning in eleven of our twelve Euroregions. Everywhere I went, members of all parties were working together to canvass and deliver leaflets, their heroic efforts compensating for the financial advantage of the other side, which could afford Royal Mail deliveries. The unfussy patriotism of those UKIP volunteers put to shame the attitude of some of their leaders.

It had been clear for some time that the success of UKIP was being bought at the expense of the wider anti-EU movement, deterring moderates and putting off floating voters. It was Sunder Katwala, director of the think tank British Future, who first came up with the phrase 'the Farage paradox' in 2014.[17] He had spotted a striking correlation in the opinion polls: the better UKIP was doing, the lower support for leaving the EU sank.

Between the start of the euro crisis in 2009 and the

17 *New Statesman*, 3 April 2014

rise of UKIP to public prominence in 2013, Leave was solidly ahead in the polls. YouGov recorded majorities of between ten and twenty-five points for most of this period. In 2010, it had Leave in front by 52 per cent to 30; in 2012 by 51 per cent to 28. That lead began to fall the following year, as UKIP stopped being lumped in with the 'Others' in BBC graphics and began to attract unprecedented coverage in the run-up to the 2014 European election. In May 2014, as UKIP secured its only ever win in a nationwide poll, Remain moved ahead for the first time. By the end of that year, there was a steady ten-point majority for staying in.

What was pushing people to a pro-EU position? It can hardly have been anything that Brussels was doing at that time. This, after all, was the period when Jean-Claude Juncker, a 1950s-style federalist, was appointed to run the European Commission despite David Cameron's furious opposition.

The explanation can be found when we drill down into the data. The slide in Eurosceptic support was most pronounced among three groups: women, ethnic minorities and, above all, young people. While we can't know for sure, it seems likely that these voters were being put off by the essentially negative way in which Euroscepticism was being promoted: not as an opportunity for a great country, but as an angry reaction to change.

The pollster Stephan Shakespeare divides the electorate into two types: 'drawbridge-uppers' and 'drawbridge-downers'. Drawbridge-uppers worry that the country is going to the dogs; drawbridge-downers believe the best is yet to come. The former regard the latter as naïve, while the latter regard the former as nasty. Each side is sometimes right.

UKIP spoke to and for the drawbridge-uppers. On every test of opinion, its voters were more nostalgic than the mean, more convinced that calamity lay ahead, readier to disbelieve statistics suggesting improvement. As Nigel Farage put it at the time: 'Voting UKIP is a state of mind.'

Now pessimism has its uses. It is an antidote to the utopianism that T. S. Eliot satirized as 'dreaming of systems so perfect that no one will need to be good'. Drawbridges may be raised for sound reasons.

But reflecting people's gripes back at them will take you only so far. Voters may share your opinion that there are too many immigrants, that welfare rules are too lax, that taxes are too high, that MPs are too lordly. But that can't be the sum of your message. You must also offer something better.

We knew that if Leave focused only on the things

that people disliked about the EU – the waste, the corruption, the lack of democracy, the open borders – we would lose. People might have agreed with us on each of those points, but the cumulative impression would be one of overwhelming negativity.

To carry the country to independence, we needed to offer a better future. We needed to talk up the global opportunities beyond the EU's restrictive customs union. We needed to focus on the advantages that would flow from being able to sign bilateral trade agreements with China, India and Australia. We needed to make an economic, democratic and optimistic case for self-rule.

That, though, was evidently not part of Nigel Farage's agenda. In order to maximize support for UKIP, he didn't need 50 per cent of the electorate; 25 per cent would do very nicely indeed. He made no effort to reach out beyond the people whose drawbridges had been raised for so long that they had rusted into place in the gatehouse. From a party political point of view, as opposed to an anti-EU one, all he needed to do was galvanize the grumpy.

He gave a series of interventions that were attention-grabbing, but that did nothing to boost the chances of a Leave vote. Complaining about foreigners with HIV using the NHS was certainly a way to make headlines, but it was hardly appealing to swing voters. Suggesting that British Muslims were fifth columnists with 'divided loyalties' might conceivably have energized part of UKIP's core vote, but what was the likely effect, in advance of the referendum, on 2 million British Muslims, many of whom had started with a natural inclination to the Commonwealth rather than the EU?

Before the 2014 European elections, I wasn't much bothered by the 'Farage paradox'. Nigel had an election to win, after all, and I hoped that, once it was out of the way, he would again work within the broader Eurosceptic movement. But it didn't happen; it didn't happen even after the 2015 general election. With no electoral contest on the horizon, UKIP's leader still seemed more interested in pumping out an angry nativist message than in trying to win the referendum.

I was personally saddened, as well as politically alarmed, by the change in Nigel's attitude. For fifteen years in the European Parliament, and in the wider *souverainiste* family, he and I had worked well together. Without his energy and single-mindedness, we wouldn't have secured the referendum at all. Because I could see that referendum on the horizon, and because I thought that we'd have to collaborate to win it, I had always made a point of being positive about Nigel in public, and in private, defending him more than once from unfair press attacks.

Shortly after the 2014 European election, his attitude shifted dramatically. He became furious when, first, two Scandinavian Eurosceptic parties and, then, a UKIP MEP, Amjad Bashir, defected to the Conservative group in the European Parliament. He blamed me for, as he bizarrely saw it, trying to destroy UKIP. In fact, in all three cases, the defectors had already made up their minds to leave, largely because they disliked Nigel's leadership style.

I didn't respond to his public rudeness, though I found it utterly bewildering. Was he seriously expecting me to turn away someone who wanted to join my party? Would he have done the same if the situation were reversed? Would anyone?

More to the point, we were about to fight a referendum on leaving the EU. After that, if all went well, there would be no more British MEPs. If our focus was on winning that referendum, it didn't matter who sat in what group in Strasbourg. As long as someone was campaigning to leave the EU, who cared what party he was in? Unless, of course, UKIP was an end in itself, and the goal of leaving the EU had become secondary.

In the event, Amjad Bashir contributed heroically

to the Leave side, campaigning day after day among Asian voters in Yorkshire and Lancashire. But this didn't stop UKIP leaders and MEPs attacking him throughout. It was clear that, at least for some of them, the party was indeed an end in itself – even at the height of the referendum campaign.

What of Nigel himself? How interested was he in winning the referendum? In November 2015, he refused to share a platform with me at an Oxford Union debate against José Manuel Barroso, insisting instead that he appear with Bill Cash. Rather than trying to reach out to the student audience, he gave his usual shtick, likening the EU to an abusive husband, and lost the vote by 283 to 73.

At the time, I thought he had formed some random and sudden aversion to me – did he honestly think it was more helpful to share a stage with George Galloway than with me? – but it turned out that everyone else was experiencing the same behaviour. Unless Nigel was centre-stage, he wouldn't co-operate. One of his aides, someone who was always studiously loyal to the leader, told me in private: 'Every single UKIP staffer and MEP recognizes what Patrick O'Flynn said about him: Nigel has become "snarling and thin-skinned". Something has happened to him and, whatever it is, it's getting worse.'

As Matthew Elliott and I and others got on with putting together the infrastructure of a referendum campaign, Nigel was focused on hounding various of his own party members. In particular, he seemed to resent two of UKIP's most effective communicators: Suzanne Evans, who had written the party's much-admired 2015 general election manifesto; and Douglas Carswell, who had evidently committed some kind of offence by winning a Westminster seat when his party leader wanted one. Even as the campaign got fully under way, Nigel was spending an inordinate amount manoeuvring to get persuasive anti-EU operators thrown out of his party.

In fact, Suzanne and Douglas may very well have saved the campaign, by taking some of the airtime to which UKIP was entitled and using it to appeal to floating voters. Had they not been in the party, and had that time been filled by other UKIP spokesmen talking about Romanians, I suspect we would have lost.

Our polling numbers were unambiguous. No Leave figure was so off-putting to undecided voters as Nigel Farage. The other side was plainly reading the same message in its own polls. Remainers did their best to make Nigel, quite literally, the face of the referendum. His were by far the most visible features in their online advertisements, and David Cameron rarely missed an opportunity to talk about 'Nigel Farage's Britain' or 'Nigel Farage and the Leave campaign'.

You didn't have to be a political scientist to see what Leave's strategy should be. Our most prominent spokesmen needed to be those to whom middle-of-the-road voters reacted well. UKIP volunteers were obviously going to be the backbone of the ground campaign; and Nigel's ideal role would be to energize and enthuse the core, rather as, say, John Prescott used to do for Labour.

These arguments cut no ice with Nigel, though. As far as he was concerned, he had to be seen to be the leader of the campaign. Whenever any cabinet minister declared for Leave, he would announce that they were welcome additions to 'my team' – hardly the best way to encourage more ministers to do the same.

To the frustration of almost everyone who wanted a Leave vote, Nigel kept predicting an easy victory based on a low participation from Remainers. It was hard to think of anything more calculated to increase turnout from the other side. Sure enough, Remain again plastered Nigel's image all over the Internet with the caption, 'Nigel Farage thinks you're not going to vote. Prove him wrong.' Yet, despite several people urging him to drop that line, he repeated it even on polling day: 'It's all about turnout and those soft Remainers staying at home.' Was he, on some subliminal level, scared of winning, and thereby putting himself and his party out of business?

Nigel was obsessed with getting into the TV debates. Naturally, Downing Street was also determined to get him into them as the face of Leave. Although the BBC was even-handed, and let the official Leave campaign put up the spokespeople it wanted, ITV allowed Number 10 to pick both sides of the debate, and staged the Cameron–Farage clash that Remainers were so desperate to bring about. It was arguably Remain's greatest tactical victory of the campaign. While it may have helped UKIP, our polls showed that it hurt Leave. The Farage paradox was becoming acute.

It is in this context that Arron Banks's aggressive and foul-mouthed attacks on Vote Leave should be seen. Perhaps Nigel and Arron could not bring themselves to believe the polls showing that a UKIP-led campaign couldn't win; perhaps they didn't care; or perhaps – it can't be ruled out – they were actually happy to lose. Some UKIP MEPs privately admitted to me that a narrow defeat was their optimum outcome, one that would allow them to return on the back of the rage of the defeated minority. They talked of it as 'the SNP strategy', a reference to the way that party had surged following its defeat in the 2014 referendum.

Not all UKIP's MEPs thought this way, of course.
Many fought the campaign honourably and full-
heartedly. And, to repeat, the party members were,
for the most part, models of disinterested patriotism.

Still, the fact that UKIP's front organization, Leave.
EU, had been brought into existence, supposedly on
an anti-EU ticket, but in reality to attack the main
Leave campaign, was a massive headache. To the
casual observer, it simply made the entire Leave side
look chaotic. Although Vote Leave never responded
to Arron Banks's increasingly deranged assaults, we
could hardly help being tarred by association.

I lost count of how many times I had variants of
the following conversation:

'You guys are a complete shower: when are you
going to stop fighting each other and concentrate
on winning?'

'We are concentrating on winning: we've just delivered four million leaflets, and we're organizing action
days on...'

'Yeah, but Banks says you're the most unpleasant
people in politics: not a good look.'

'Like I say, we're concentrating on our campaign. We've just launched Bangladeshis for Britain, and we...'

'Then why are you fighting like ferrets in a sack?'

'We're not fighting; we're not responding to Leave.EU. We're concentrating on winning the vote. What is it you'd like us to be doing differently?'

'Well, I don't know, but the overall impression is awful. And another thing: can't you stop using Nigel Farage?'

I had that conversation, in various forms, not just with journalists, but with many potential supporters and contributors. Perhaps the single most damaging consequence of the Leave.EU spoiler operation was that it deterred donors from offering support until it was clear which group would win designation as the official Leave campaign – by which time, the statutory spending caps were operational. While Remain made full use of the pre-designation period to spend before the limits came into effect, sending out several leaflets expensively by post, we had to rely on a network of local volunteers to stuff material through letterboxes.

Pro-EU campaigners couldn't believe their luck. Here was an organization dedicated to sabotaging the main Leave operation, but that successfully presented itself as Eurosceptic. Along with all the other logistical advantages Remain enjoyed – the support of the big corporates and the big political parties, the massive financial lead, the readiness to extend the voter registration period, the active participation of the machinery of state, the spending of £9.3 million of taxpayers' money on pro-EU propaganda – it seemed to make a Remain victory almost inevitable. Small wonder that the betting was heavily on Remain throughout. Small wonder that, even on polling day, Remain tacticians were looking forward to a 60–40 victory.

Why didn't it happen? Ultimately, because Leave had the better song to sing. Had our campaign truly been the anti-immigrant, nostalgic one that some Remainers now allege, we'd never have come close. The numbers speak for themselves. No fewer than 17,410,742 people voted Leave – more than have voted for anything else, ever. But UKIP's vote at the last election was 3,881,129. In other words, something like four in five Leave voters were not UKIP supporters. Had our message been essentially negative, there is simply no way we could have won. We carried people with us by being upbeat throughout.

Remain, by contrast, locked itself into a campaign of fear and pessimism. Leaving would mean migrant camps in Kent and no trade deals and emergency tax rises and punishment budgets and blah blah fishcakes. Undecided voters found Leave the more cheerful of the two campaigns, and were commensurately ready to give us their sympathetic attention.

We also had the better political operation. Early on, Matthew asked me what I thought about approaching Dominic Cummings to be our campaign director. I told him that it was his call but that, for what it was worth, I had known Dom for more than twenty years and could think of no more effective street-fighter.

Dom's approach to data and demographic targeting was revolutionary. Lacking the resources of the other side, he found some brilliant astrophysicists who had ways of scraping data from people's online profiles and building up a picture of who and where our likely voters were. The more data we could feed into their model, the more accurate it became.

Dom's radical tactics meant that I had to spend quite a lot of time during the campaign reassuring our volunteers that the canvassing they were doing was invaluable. They, naturally enough, couldn't understand why we needed canvass returns when we weren't in a position to reach more than a tiny fraction of the electorate. Why not spend the time leafleting instead? 'Trust me, chaps, we have this very clever man who sits at a huge computer. Every canvass return you give him makes that computer work better. I can't put it any more clearly than that, because I'm no tech expert, but I promise you he knows what he's doing.'

He did. Our knocking-up operation, which started five days before the poll, was superb: we knew exactly whom to target. The Remain operation, by contrast, was pedestrian, even amateurish. It was very curious. Remainers had hired an American campaigner called Jim Messina, who had worked wonders for Barack Obama, and whose speciality was finding out exactly how to approach target groups of voters – women in their forties, say, or self-employed people, or members of wine clubs or whatever – and to deluge those voters with messages tailored specifically to them, right down to the font on the envelope. I kept waiting for the waves of recipient-specific Messina communications; but they never came.

A lot of people have since criticized Dom in particular, and the campaign more generally, for fighting dirty. Most of all, we are excoriated for quoting Britain's gross contribution the EU budget – £350 million a week – rather than the net figure, which takes account of the rebate and the money spent in the UK.

I don't accept that criticism. It's normal, in public life, to quote gross rather than net contributions. Suppose I were to ask you what the basic rate of income tax was. Would you tell me that it was 20p in the pound, or would you say, 'Actually, if you think about it, it's zero, because we get it all back in roads, schools and hospitals'?

We also knew, though, that quoting the gross figure might tempt some of the less disciplined Remainers into an argument about precisely how many million pounds we sent over to Brussels each week. That was an argument that they couldn't win; as long as the focus of the debate was on our financial tribute to the EU, we were picking up votes. In the event, it wasn't just one or two novice Remain campaigners who made this mistake; it was their campaign as a whole. We thanked our lucky stars.

Naturally enough, some of the losers now blame the man who defeated them. And, in fairness, even Dom's best friends will concede that he doesn't always go out of his way to charm people. But it was a competitive referendum, for Heaven's sake. In any such campaign, you run with your strongest messages. Provided you don't tell lies, it makes sense to emphasize the arguments that matter most to undecided voters. Dom was brought in as a campaign director, not as a flower arranger. His job was not to win elegantly; it was to win.

As the campaign got under way, the Vote Leave HQ, in an office block on the Albert Embankment, filled up with young people, many of whom worked solidly from Christmas 2015 until polling day, with barely a Sunday off. What we lacked in celebrity endorsements, political professionals and big money, we more than made up for in passion and commitment. I will remember until my last day on Earth the sheer energy and selflessness of those staffers.

By the time six cabinet ministers declared for Leave, an operation was already in progress nationwide, with activists answering to regional directors, local press teams, local business networks and, exactly as Matt and I had discussed nearly four years earlier, a series of sectoral campaign groups: Students for Britain, Africans for Britain, Bikers for Britain, Kiwis for Britain, Out and Proud (our LGBT group), Green Leaves, Economists for Brexit, Women for Britain and so on. I spent much of the referendum campaigning with Muslims for Britain, a brilliantly effective group run largely by some second-generation Brits of Pakistani origin in the West Midlands. Their leafleting in mosques and community centres probably tipped the balance in Birmingham.

There will, no doubt, be some accounts of the campaign published this year by journalists, a first draft of history, as it were. Then there will be dozens of Ph.D. theses, some of which will eventually turn up as academic books. All will rightly give credit to the professional team, to the Vote Leave staff, to the sympathetic writers and journalists, to our business backers and to the politicians who fronted the campaign: Boris Johnson, Gisela Stuart, Anthony Bamford, Iain Duncan Smith, Michael Gove, Priti Patel, Dominic Raab, Ian Davidson, Bernard Jenkin, Chris Grayling, Andrea Leadsom, John Longworth, Liam Fox, Kate Hoey, Nigel Lawson, Michael Forsyth, Owen Paterson – all, all honourable men and women.

I can't finish this section, though, without mentioning two more people who can genuinely claim to have tipped the result but who – unless those Ph.D. students are uncommonly good investigative reporters – won't get anything like the recognition they deserve.

In a world where some politicians see Euroscepticism almost as a test of virility, Theresa Villiers has always been stunningly modest. Her first act as Transport Secretary was to remove the EU flag from all her department's buildings – something I discovered much later, and quite by chance, from one of her civil servants. Can you think of any other politician, certainly any male politician, who would make such a gesture *and then not tell anyone*?

On more than one occasion, while other Eurosceptics postured, she acted, unremarked and unreported. When she politely made clear that she couldn't support the PM's deal in Brussels, it mattered. David Cameron decided that she would be allowed to campaign for a Leave vote without having to resign from the cabinet. Once that decision was known, it became far easier for other ministers to declare for Leave. Had Theresa, along with Chris Grayling, not extracted that concession early, I'm not sure we'd have won.

If the number of ministers who came out for Leave surprised Downing Street, the total number of Conservative MPs doing so caused real consternation. Number 10 had expected thirty or forty MPs to campaign against EU membership. In the event, according to the definitive list compiled by the ConservativeHome website, 128 Tory MPs campaigned to quit the EU – 40 per cent of all those who declared their position. Euroscepticism, a minority pursuit in the parliamentary Conservative party until that point, had suddenly become mainstream.

There were various factors at work. Some MPs were responding to pressure from their activists. Others had concluded, after the failure of David Cameron's renegotiation, that the EU could never reform. But much of the credit for those numbers must go to Steve Baker, the likeable and quietly religious MP for Wycombe who had, until then, been mainly known for his relentless campaigns against loose monetary policy. Steve now likes to tease me about the rather clumsy way in which I asked him to take on the role:

'Do you remember what you said to me, Dan?'

'I'm sure I said you were the perfect man for the job, Steve. It's certainly what I was thinking.'

'No. Your exact words were: "There's no one else who can do it."'

Well, there wasn't. I had first supposed that, when the moment came, the parliamentary side of the campaign would be organized by David Heathcoat-Amory, a respected former minister. But David unexpectedly lost his seat at the 2010 election. Then, I assumed that the job would fall to Douglas Carswell and Mark Reckless, but both of them had defected to UKIP.

Despite my graceless approach, Steve cheerfully agreed to run Conservatives for Britain, which marshalled party members as well as MPs, and which ended up providing many of the volunteers who ran our ground operation. Steve was able to get even the prickliest MPs to accept his chairmanship, largely because he has oceanic reserves of patience and courtesy, and is always happy to let others hog the headlines. Which, of course, is why he, too, hasn't received anything like the recognition he earned. Nor have the other early Tory Leavers who prepared the ground for the rest of the party: Anne-Marie Trevelyan, James Cleverly, Jacob Rees-Mogg, Bill Wiggin.

I could fill the rest of this book with acknowledgements. But I hope I have given enough of a flavour of the main actors, both during the pre-campaign period and during the referendum itself, to make at least one thing clear: the chief motivation of British Eurosceptics, going right back to the 1975 campaign, has been a desire to restore parliamentary supremacy and the right to make our own laws.

For whatever reason, the government never seemed to believe it. David Cameron based his renegotiation on trying to get better terms on migration and benefits – and then failed to get even that. But he never sought to get a substantively better deal on sovereignty, the issue which Michael Gove and Boris Johnson had both identified, publicly and privately, as the determining factor.

Even had he secured a better deal on migration – a total ban on benefits, say, or an emergency brake on numbers – it would probably not have changed the outcome. What people wanted was control over our national affairs. A deal that put Britain back in charge overall would, as it were, incidentally have addressed concerns over immigration. It is one thing to have a bilateral deal with a friendly country providing for reciprocal rights of work or study; quite another to have a foreign court telling you whom to admit, on what terms, and with what entitlements.

Yet still this point doesn't seem to have sunk in. 'We know what people voted against,' say pundits, 'but it's far from clear what they voted for.' Actually, it's totally clear: they voted to leave the EU and take back control of their own laws. They didn't dictate exactly what kind of deal we should have with our neighbours after leaving – that is for ministers to negotiate; but they instructed those ministers to base the relationship on collaboration rather than coercion, alliance rather than amalgamation, sovereignty rather than subordination.

When Leave campaigners invited people to 'take back control', we meant precisely that: that legal supremacy should return from Brussels to Westminster.

Remainers never wanted to concede that sovereignty was an issue. They spent the campaign trying to suggest that the EU was just one among several international associations in which Britain participated. It was, they wanted us to believe, a club, like NATO or the G20, through which we agreed to abide by common rules in order to secure common objectives. All such associations, they argued, involved some loss of sovereignty. If we wanted 'undiluted sovereignty', averred Sir John Major, we should 'go to North Korea'.

Not for the first time, Sir John badly underestimated the electorate. People could see that the EU differed from every other international body in that it presumed to legislate for its member states. Membership of NATO or the G20 may mean ceding *power* in certain areas, but it emphatically doesn't mean ceding *sovereignty* – that is, the ultimate right to determine laws.

If NATO or the G20 aspired to unitary statehood, they, too, might become subjects of referendums. So far, though, no other body in the world has awarded itself supreme legal authority. I write 'awarded itself' deliberately. The primacy of EU law was not in the

Treaty of Rome. Rather, as even committed federalists admit, it was invented by the ECJ in a series of expansive judgments in 1963 and 1964.

Since then, the EU's treaties have been unlike any other international accords. Instead of binding their signatories as states, they sustain a separate legal order, superior to national laws and directly binding upon businesses and individuals *within* states. In any conflict between a parliamentary statute and a ruling by the ECJ, our courts automatically uphold the latter.

The EU has steadily enlarged its powers, most recently by adopting the Charter of Fundamental Rights and Freedoms, which allows the ECJ to rule on almost every aspect of national life. When the Blair government signed up to the charter, ministers dismissed it as no more justiciable than the *Beano*. Yet it is now being used by Abu Hamza's daughter-in-law to challenge her deportation from the UK on the grounds that her son is an EU citizen.

When people read of such cases, they know that it is idiotic to describe the EU as a club. In the 1970s, Lord Denning likened European law to an incoming tide, pushing against the flow of our rivers, causing them to burst their banks. In 1990, toward the end of his rich life, he revised his metaphor:

No longer is European law an incoming tide flowing up the estuaries of England. It is now like a tidal wave bringing down our sea walls and flowing inland over our fields and houses – to the dismay of all.

On 23 June 2016, people voted to restore Britain's political independence. This point is worth stressing because, since the poll, several Remain supporters have become overnight experts on what the other side 'really' wanted. Leavers, we keep being told, were voting against immigration, or against political elites, or against inequality – against anything, in fact, except the EU membership specified on the ballot paper.

Next to the various theories offered by columnists, we have one hard and massive data set. On polling day, Lord Ashcroft's field workers asked 12,369 people why they had just voted as they had. The answer was unequivocal. By far the biggest motivation for Leave voters was 'the principle that decisions about the UK should be taken in the UK', with 49 per cent support. Control of immigration was a distant second on 33 per cent.[18]

Other polls produced similar results. A ComRes survey in the *Sunday Mirror* found that sovereignty

18 Lord Ashcroft Polls, 24 June 2016

had been the main motivation for 53 per cent of Leave voters, immigration for 34 per cent.[19]

Addressing the concern of the main group of Leave voters is, on one level, very straightforward. Parliament simply has to repeal Sections 2 and 3 of the 1972 European Communities Act – the clauses that provide for EU law to take precedence over UK law.

The sensitivities around repeal are not legal but diplomatic. How can we carry out that abrogation while retaining the goodwill of our allies? Might we, for example, replicate some of our existing EU obligations through bilateral treaties, either open-endedly or for a guaranteed period? Should we aim at a hard exit, opting out of most EU regulations and becoming as Singapore to the EU's Malaysia? Or a soft exit, keeping the bulk of the existing arrangements and continuing to adopt many of the same standards as our neighbours for reasons of economy of scale? Or something in between the two? Or something else entirely?

19 ComRes, 26 June 2012

3

A EUROPEAN FREE-TRADE AREA

THE EUROPEAN PROBLEM – or from a Brussels perspective, the British problem – can be very easily stated. The United Kingdom wants to trade freely with its European neighbours, not to amalgamate with them politically.

The trouble is, the option of 'trade only' was initially not on the menu. Joining meant signing up to something much more than a market. It meant accepting a European political identity. In 1950, as the six original EEC members began to discuss the merger of their institutions, Britain's foreign secretary, the plain-talking trade unionist, Ernest Bevin, explained why there was no appetite to join them: 'Britain is not part of Europe, she is simply not a Luxembourg.'[20]

As political integration got under way on the Continent following the 1951 Paris Treaty, which established the European Coal and Steel Community, Britain kept trying to steer Europe in a different direction. The Attlee, Churchill and Eden governments urged neighbouring states to form a broad free-trade area that would remain open to the rest of the world, and that would concern itself with commerce rather than integration.

While they accepted that some European states might want to federate, their hope was that any such bloc might take shape within a larger common market, based on the eighteen-member Organization for European Economic Co-operation (the forerunner to today's OECD), which covered almost the whole of Europe outside the Soviet bloc.

The critical difference was this: while Britain wanted a free-trade area that would remain open to the United States, the Commonwealth and the developing world, federalists in France, Germany, Italy and the Benelux states wanted a customs union.

This distinction might sound technical, but it is absolutely critical to understanding what Britain will

20 Quoted in *Facts are Subversive* by Timothy Garton Ash

do in the months ahead, so we should take a moment to consider the difference. A free-trade area is a group of states which have eliminated most or all tariffs and quotas on their trade. Sometimes their agreement covers only manufactured goods and commodities. Sometimes it applies to services, too. In a few cases, it incorporates free movement of labour. Examples of free-trade areas are EFTA (Iceland, Norway, Switzerland and Liechtenstein), NAFTA (Canada, the United States and Mexico) and ASEAN (ten South East Asian states).

A customs union, by contrast, involves internal free trade, but also a common external tariff. Its members surrender their separate commercial policies, and give up the right to sign trade agreements. Instead, trade negotiations are conducted, and treaties signed, by the bloc as a whole. Customs unions often exist where one state administers another, or where a tiny nation contracts out its trade policy to a larger neighbour: Swaziland and Lesotho are in a customs union with South Africa; Israel with the Palestinian territories. Other than the EU, the three chief customs unions on the planet are Mercosur and the Andean Community – both of which were created after heavy lobbying by the EU, which made clear that it would not sign worthwhile trade or aid deals with individual countries, but would deal only bloc-to-bloc – and the Eurasian Union, which ties Armenia, Belarus, Kazakhstan and Kyrgyzstan to Russia.

One way to think of the difference is this: NAFTA, being a free-trade area, could accept Britain, while allowing it to make its own trade deals with the EU. But the reverse is not true: the EU, being a customs union, insists on exclusivity.

Economists generally prefer free-trade areas to customs unions, because they facilitate global trade and promote competition. On the other hand, customs unions are a better way to encourage political integration.

Britain's efforts to haul the Continent in a more liberal direction in the 1950s failed. As far as the leaders of the Six were concerned, the key aim was political unification, which they believed, sincerely if incorrectly, to be the answer to the two dreadful wars through which they had lived. Hence their determination to begin with coal and steel – without which war was thought to be impossible.

Economics was subordinated to politics. Or, if you prefer, economic integration was seen as a way to build a United States of Europe, rather than as a way to make people better off. Right from the start, it was decided that a high tariff wall, along with a common industrial policy and a common agricultural policy, would mesh the participating states more closely together.

For free-trading Britain, with its global supply lines and habit of importing food and commodities from the Commonwealth, such policies were unthinkable. The UK sought to separate the issue of commerce from that of political federation – that is, to encourage the countries that wanted to merge their institutions to do so as a sub-unit within a much larger pan-European free-trade area.

At the Messina summit in 1955, a British official made a final – by then, rather perfunctory – effort to advance this idea, known in the Foreign Office as 'Plan G'. His arguments served only to convince the foreign ministers of the Six that they needed to push ahead immediately, before Britain's alternative plan could gain traction.[21]

In 1957, the Six formed the European Economic Community. Its foundational text, the Treaty of Rome, committed the signatories to establish an 'ever-closer union', and its articles provided for the development of a Common Commercial Policy based on a Common External Tariff.

Although Britain continued to discuss the possibility

21 Martin Schaad, *Contemporary European History*, 1998

of membership, the talks had a somewhat desultory quality. Britain was a major importer of food and commodities from the Commonwealth and South America. No British government could accept the Common Agricultural Policy or the Common External Tariff – let alone the goal of eventual federation.

In 1960, Britain took the lead in setting up a more comfortable bloc – the European Free Trade Association (EFTA) – along with Norway, Sweden, Denmark, Austria, Switzerland and her oldest ally, Portugal. Unlike the EEC, EFTA had no interest in political amalgamation. And, unlike the EEC, it was not a customs union but a free-trade area.

The division of Western Europe into two rival but friendly groupings might have lasted indefinitely, but for Edward Heath's implausible election as prime minister in 1970. No senior British politician, before or since, has had Heath's obsession with building a United States of Europe. Having been the chief negotiator during Harold Macmillan's unsuccessful entry bid, he was determined to get in on any terms, and the Six knew it.

Heath dropped all the objections that previous administrations had had to the external tariff wall, to the exclusion of Commonwealth produce and to the *finalité politique*. He threw in Britain's rich fishing

grounds as a sort of late-entry fee. He was even prepared
to accept that the EEC should keep its existing four
working languages – only lobbying by Ireland, which
was applying to join at the same time, ensured that
English had the same status as French, German, Dutch
and Italian.

Indeed, the only significant concession won by
Britain in those talks was that it should retain its commercial relationship with its EFTA partners. Obviously,
since it was now joining the EEC's Common External
Tariff, this meant that the EEC as a whole had to agree
to free trade with EFTA.

The defection of the United Kingdom left EFTA
with no large member state, and so altered the balance
of Europe. Denmark, always close to Britain economically, politically and culturally, joined the EEC on
the same day, 1 January 1973. Portugal followed in
1986, and Austria and Sweden in 1994. In each case,
the new EEC members retained their trade links with
their former EFTA partners, but had to take on a series
of new responsibilities, both in terms of economic and
non-economic regulation.

EFTA still exists, and still regulates its members'
trade relations separately from the EU. Under the EFTA
treaty, known as the Vaduz Convention, the four remaining EFTA states – Iceland, Norway, Switzerland and

Liechtenstein – agree to maintain among themselves free movement of goods, services, labour and capital.

There is, though, a significant difference between Switzerland and the other three EFTA states as regards how they relate to the EU. On 1 January 1994, Norway, Iceland and Liechtenstein joined the European Economic Area (EEA), intended as a prelude to full EU membership. Switzerland, following a close referendum at the end of 1992, stayed out.

During the recent British referendum, Remain campaigners made much of the supposed disadvantages of the EEA arrangement and, although some of their claims were exaggerated, and some downright untrue, the EEA does have its drawbacks.

Before coming to those drawbacks, it's worth noting that the EEA states enjoy more freedom and sovereignty than Britain does as an EU member. The EEA Agreement covers most aspects of the EU's single market, but not criminal justice, agriculture, fisheries, foreign affairs, non-EU trade, defence or large chunks of environmental policy.

It's worth noting, too, that most people in EEA states are content with their current arrangements. Voters in Norway, Iceland and Liechtenstein oppose EU membership by large and settled majorities. In Norway, there has been no pro-accession opinion poll while the EEA has existed and, since 2010, opponents have enjoyed leads of two-to-one or more. In Iceland, there was a slight wobble during the financial crash, but the Eurosceptics resumed their solid lead within months as the initial crisis subsided – and, indeed, as the days lengthened, which, in my experience, always lifts the mood in Iceland.

Icelanders could see that being outside the EU had allowed them to recuperate, despite the proportionate vastness of their banks' liabilities. 'I am pretty sure our recovery couldn't have happened if we had been part of the EU,' said the then prime minister, Sigmundur Davíð Gunnlaugsson of the centrist Progressive Party. 'We might have gone the other way and become a bankrupt country.' Icelanders, he added, had only to look at Ireland, Greece and other EU states to see what their fate might have been.

The EEA states outperform the EU on almost every measure. They have higher GDP per head, higher rates of employment, lower inflation and stronger growth. They also do better on non-economic indicators. The United Nations runs a quality-of-life index, which measures literacy, longevity, infant mortality and the like. Norway is in the top position – with Switzerland in third place, after Australia.

Not such a frightening prospect, you might think.

Yet Norway was constantly on the lips of pro-EU campaigners as an example of what not to do. David Cameron even launched the Remain campaign by warning against what he called a 'Norway-style future'.[22] Oddly enough, he did so, not in Norway, but in Iceland, where he was attending a summit meeting. Although Iceland and Norway were both EEA members, and had similar deals with Brussels, the Norwegian political class was and is pro-EU, whereas most Icelanders were longing for Britain to rejoin EFTA. Remain campaigners therefore always spoke of 'Norway' when they meant the EEA.

The PM outlined three objections to 'the Norwegian model'. First, that Norway and the other EEA states 'still have to follow EU rules but with no votes or say over how they are set'. Second, that 'Norway has to pay hundreds of millions of euros in membership fees to access the single market'. Third, that 'Norway has to fully accept the principle of free movement of people' – though he didn't explain why this was any worse than what the UK was already doing.

Let's consider these three objections in order.

It's true that EEA states have to follow some EU rules, though nothing like as many as has been claimed. Throughout the referendum campaign, Stronger In

22 *Daily Telegraph*, 28 October 2016

maintained that Norway had to apply '75 per cent of EU laws'. In the heat of debate, its spokesmen often went further, risibly claiming that Norway had to apply 'almost all' or even 'all' EU laws.

What is the actual figure? Using the EFTA Secretariat's official statistics, a study found that between 2000 and 2013, Norway applied 4,724 EU legal instruments. Over the same period, the EU itself adopted 52,183 legal instruments. That's not 75 per cent; it's 9 per cent.[23]

The figure is similar across the EEA. In reply to a parliamentary question, the Icelandic government declared that between 1994 and 2014, it had adopted 6,326 of 62,809 EU legal acts – 10 per cent.[24]

So where did the 75-per-cent figure come from? It turned out to have originated in a paper produced for the former leader of Norway's European Movement. It was based, not on any empirical method, but on a more or less intuitive estimate. It applied only to EU directives, not to regulations or other legal acts. Oddly, it came only in the English-language foreword, not the Norwegian original. And it was phrased as 'approximately three quarters' – British Remainers

23 NtEU Fakta, Morten Harper, 4 March 2016
24 Reply by foreign minister Gunnar Bragi Sveinsson to Guðlaugur Þór Þórðarson, 21 October 2015

decided to render it as '75 per cent', presumably so as to give it an air of forensic precision.

Still, while the real figure may be closer to 9 per cent, it is none the less true to say that Norway has no formal role in the legislative process relating to that fraction of its laws. That's not to say, of course, that it has no voice. The EEA agreement provides for consultative mechanisms for the non-EU states in the pre-legislative stage. As Anne Tvinnereim, a former minister from Norway's Centre Party, explains: 'We are not there when they vote, but we do get to influence the position. Most of the politics is done long before it gets to the voting stage.'[25]

More to the point, though, Norway is not subject to the direct effect of EU laws. It doesn't have any mechanism, as Britain has, for Brussels decisions to become immediately binding on its territory. EU laws have force in Norway only after they have been passed in Norway's parliament, the Storting.

It's true that Norway's Europhile ministers have tended to transcribe anything that comes their way, but the EEA treaty provides for a 'right of reservation'. When, for example, Norway didn't like the EU's Postal Services Directive, it declined to implement it.

So, while it is true that Norway must take, at

25 EUreferendum.com, 1 August 2013

second hand, some EU legal acts, the problem is far greater in theory than in practice. Those acts are proportionately few; Norway gets an informal say rather than the minuscule vote it would get as an EU state with 5 million people; and, in an extreme case, Norway can simply decline to pass the requisite implementing legislation in its own parliament.

What of David Cameron's second objection, namely that Norway has to pay for access to the single market? It's true that under the terms of the EEA Norway pays a certain amount – as, of course, all countries do when they belong to international associations. Norway also pays a share of the administrative costs of Schengen, the border-free area in which, unlike the UK, it participates. Norway opts in to a number of other European schemes, such as Erasmus, the university exchange programme, and Horizon 2020, the joint research fund. Obviously, it pays into these programmes in return for the right to participate. It doesn't have to pay into the single largest element of the EU budget, namely the CAP. But it has agreed to make a contribution to the funds that are supposed to build up infrastructure in the EU's less developed regions.

How do Norway's contributions compare to the UK's? The EU itself does not produce a like-for-like comparison, and there are, as we saw during the recent campaign, many different ways of calculating a country's EU budget payments. The most comprehensive study of the balance for EU and EFTA states was carried out by Professor Herman Matthijs of the Free University of Brussels. He found that Iceland's annual per capita contribution is 50 euros, Switzerland's 68 and Norway's 107. Britain's current payment, by the same methodology, is 229 euros.

In other words, all the alternatives are significantly cheaper than what Britain is doing now. How much cheaper will depend on how many of the EU's policies we want to remain involved with. Some years ago, when writing a paper on EFTA, I asked government officials in both Oslo and Reykjavík why Iceland paid so much less than Norway, given that both had signed up to the same EEA terms. The Norwegian officials gave me some lengthy explanations about how important the EU's aid, research and development programmes were. The Icelanders grinned broadly and said, 'Sometimes our Norwegian friends can be completely f***ing crazy.'

It's David Cameron's third objection, free movement, that has become the focus of media attention since the vote. We are repeatedly told that the four freedoms of the single market are indivisible, that we can't have free movement of goods, services and capital unless we have free movement of people, too.

As a matter of fact, this isn't true. Of the three states in the EEA, two have signed up to the unrestricted free movement of EU nationals for the purposes of employment, and one, Liechtenstein, has negotiated the right to cap numbers. By agreement with the EU, Liechtenstein admits 71 European migrants per year. My point is not that Britain is comparable to the princely microstate; it's simply to show that the EU does not regard the four freedoms as inseparable, whatever its spokesmen now claim.

In any case, there is a difference between the free movement of labour and the free movement of persons. Free movement of labour was indeed one of the foundational principles of the EEC, and Britain signed up to it when it joined. Free movement of labour meant the right to take up a job offer in another member state. A Briton with a job in Paris could turn up to the local commune with a copy of his employment contract and be issued with the necessary residence papers.

The rules changed, as in so many aspects of European policy, when the Maastricht Treaty came into effect. Maastricht created a new constitutional status: 'citizenship of the European Union'. EU citizenship bestowed legal entitlements, enforceable by the ECJ, including the rights to reside anywhere in the EU, to vote at local or European elections in any member state and to non-discrimination on grounds of nationality. It is this last which has been almost open-endedly interpreted, as its authors evidently intended, to mean equal access to benefits, subsidized university places and the like.

Whatever else it means, leaving the EU must mean ceasing to be EU citizens. The arrangements we negotiate on migration, whether or not they involve reciprocal rights of work and study, will be secured through bilateral treaties, not through European jurisdiction. This change may sound technical, but its implications are vast. Many of the extensions of EU competence in the field of benefits have come about through judicial activism rather than through treaty change. New and expensive rights on welfare and pension entitlements have been determined, in effect, by the ECJ, not by the member states.

Even if the UK did nothing beyond withdrawing from the jurisdiction of the ECJ and replicating its current deals bilaterally, that would still be a considerable gain, because it would prevent further 'competence creep' – that is, the stealthy extension of EU jurisdiction beyond what was originally agreed.

In practice, of course, the UK should not replicate all its existing deals: most voters want to find ways to control inward migration, while giving due weight to the interests of our European allies and due consideration to the advantages of reciprocity. I'm simply making the point that ceasing to be Citizens of the European Union is a substantive rather than a symbolic gain.

Reinstating the requirement that you find a job before moving would likewise make a significant difference: around 70,000 EU nationals enter Britain every year looking for work.

A moratorium on all benefits claims for an initial period of four or five years would also be much more than symbolic. Many EU nationals come to the UK looking to save up a lump sum, often with a view to buying their first home. Removing in-work benefits would make that prospect far less appealing.

All these are ways in which inward migration can be regulated without breaching the broad principle of free movement of labour. Applying them would mean, in practice, a decline in the number of unskilled workers entering the UK, but not of skilled workers. This is, incidentally, what most British voters say they want. Only 12 per cent want fewer qualified workers from the EU.[26]

26 Poll for British Future, 22 August 2016

My point is not to set out precisely what our post-EU migration policy should be; it is simply to demonstrate that it is perfectly possible to negotiate some constraints on the unrestricted movement of people without prejudicing the free movement of goods, services and capital.

In summary, then, EEA countries have a far better deal than do existing EU states. They have legal supremacy on their own territory. They can sign trade deals with non-EU states. They apply only a minority of EU rules. They pay less into the EU budget than do the member states. They are not obliged to participate in any measures outside the fields of trade and economics, though they sometimes choose to opt in. And they are outside the Common Agricultural Policy and the Common Fisheries Policy, both of which disproportionately penalize the United Kingdom.

Still, their arrangements are not ideal. In particular, they are obliged, with some small exemptions, to apply EU technical standards to the whole of their economies, not just to those things they are exporting to the EU.

This, rather than migration, is what makes EEA membership unattractive. As we have seen, a precedent exists to combine EEA membership with limits on inward migration. Britain could, no doubt, negotiate some further restrictions on migration while remaining in the single market. But membership of, as opposed to access to, the single market, is costly. Britain ought not to accept, in the long term, the requirement to apply EU regulations to the 85 per cent of its economy that does not depend on EU trade, being accounted for instead either by trade with the rest of the world or by wholly domestic activity.

It is worth noting that the 85-per-cent figure is far higher for the UK than it is for any of the EEA states. In per-capita terms, Britain exports less than half as much to the EU than does Norway. While a case can be made for Norway, with 1 per cent of the EU's population, to adopt the same standards as its chief customers, that argument is far weaker in Britain, which exports less in proportionate terms, and whose exports mainly go outside the EU.

So, on balance, it makes little sense for the UK to remain in the EEA, other than possibly as a very short-term transitional measure. Incidentally, 'remain in the EEA' is the accurate term. There has been much discussion in the press about whether we might 'join' the EEA on leaving the EU, but we are already members, having acceded as an individual signatory in 1994, along with the other EU and EFTA states. Leaving the EU will not automatically annul our EEA membership; we shall have to resign separately from both organizations.

EFTA, however, is an altogether less intrusive arrangement, and one which we ought seriously to consider. The difference between Switzerland and the three EFTA states which also joined the EEA stems from that country's magnificent tradition of direct democracy. When Swiss voters rejected EEA membership in a referendum, narrow as the result was, Swiss politicians unhesitatingly accepted the verdict and sat down to negotiate alternative arrangements with the EU.

Over the next few years, Switzerland negotiated around 200 sectoral treaties, covering everything from fish farming to the permitted noise of lorries on the highways. These are bilateral treaties. There is no way for the EU to enforce its rulings on Switzerland as it can on Slovenia, Spain or Sweden. However, they are not all free-standing treaties. Switzerland has accepted that some of them depend upon others, and that withdrawing from one area would automatically annul a number of others.

This is relevant to the current British debate, not least with reference to the question of migration. Switzerland has signed a bilateral deal with the EU providing for reciprocal free movement. On 9 February

2014, in response to a popular initiative, the Swiss voted in a referendum to impose some limits on EU migration. The margin was very narrow – 50.3 per cent to 49.7 per cent – and the proposition was more mildly worded than the surrounding press coverage often implied. It merely mandated the federal government in Berne to negotiate *some* limits on free movement within the following three years.

This did not seem an impossible task and, although the initial reaction in Brussels to the Swiss vote was somewhat petulant, the two sides sat down amicably enough to discuss terms. By the beginning of 2015, those close to the talks were optimistic that the broad outlines of a deal had been agreed – a deal that, while it might fall short of what some Swiss wanted, would at least provide for a measure of control.

Then came David Cameron's unexpected victory in the 2015 general election, and the unwelcome realization (in Brussels) that Britain really was going to go through with its referendum on leaving. Suddenly, the Swiss talks stalled. 'We were basically there,' a Swiss diplomat told me at the time, 'but then your referendum intervened. The EU side didn't want British voters to see that Switzerland could get a good deal on migration.'

And so Switzerland, at the time of writing, has not

reached a final settlement, though voices there are being raised in favour of forming a joint negotiating position with London. In the meantime, Switzerland and the EU appear to be reaching a compromise that would allow the Swiss government to give precedence to its own nationals in employment.

Let me repeat once more, as I did a thousand times during the campaign: the United Kingdom is not going precisely to mimic the arrangements of any other state. In constantly asking whether we wanted Britain to be 'like' Norway or 'like' Switzerland or 'like' Jersey or 'like' Canada, the Remain side illustrated the silliness of the question. The fact that no two non-EU states had identical deals with Brussels ought to have told us that Britain, just like any of them, would strike its own bargain, tailored to suit its own conditions and needs.

None the less, the idea of having EFTA-style trading relations with the EU, without the obligations of EEA membership, is an appealing one.

To make a couple of obvious points, Switzerland is doing extremely well as an EFTA-only state, and its people plainly prefer its current status to the EEA, let alone full EU membership.

Switzerland vies with Norway at the top of the prosperity indices. Its economy is truly global: as well as its comprehensive free-trade agreement with the EU, it has agreements with China, Japan and other large economies. The Swiss export £29,298 per head as against £5,277 for the UK. They are wealthier, too: GDP per capita is £60,403 to Britain's £32,663. Wages are higher by a similar factor, and taxes are lower.

Swiss unemployment is historically and structurally low – currently 4.5 per cent compared to an EU rate of 10.2 per cent; and its companies are world-beating – Nestlé and Novartis, Rolex and Swatch, Glencore and UBS.

Perhaps unsurprisingly, in the circumstances, very few Swiss want to join the EU. Opinion polls on the issue have become uncommon, because the EU issue was widely seen to have been killed off when 76.8 per cent of Swiss voted 'No' in a referendum in 2001. Still, for what it's worth, the last published survey, from 2015, shows that 82 per cent of voters prefer their current deal to membership.

It's true that the deal between Switzerland and the EU is imperfect: treaties are necessarily imperfect, being the result of protracted talks between flawed negotiators. The main drawback is that Switzerland has allowed its various arrangements with the EU to become interlinked, so that withdrawing from one means that others are automatically abrogated.

The United Kingdom should seek to avoid that mistake in its talks with the EU.

A second disadvantage, much cited by Remain during the late campaign, is that Switzerland is largely outside the single market in financial services. While this may be true, one can't help noticing that Switzerland none the less has a flourishing financial sector. Its banks and other services must operate under a different regulatory regime when selling in the EU, but the flip side is that they are exempt from EU rules. The Swiss don't need to worry about the short-selling ban or the bonus cap or the Alternative Investment Fund Managers Directive or the Financial Transactions Tax. Indeed, following the EU's heavy-handed regulation of fund management, many companies relocated from London to Zug.

There is a strong case for short circuiting a number of issues by resuming our seat at EFTA. First, and most obviously, it would guarantee our continued free trade with the other EFTA states. It's true that signing up to the Vaduz Convention would also mean reciprocal free movement of people with Norway, Switzerland and Iceland but, given the size of these countries' populations and their income per capita, it is hard to see anyone objecting in principle to such an arrangement.

Second, although EFTA allows its member states to negotiate their own trade deals with third countries (Iceland and Switzerland have FTAs with China, while Norway stands aside on human-rights grounds), it sometimes negotiates as a bloc for the sake of convenience. Its resulting trade deals are far more impressive than those of the EU.

The EU's trade deals are limited and local in their ambition. Most of them are with the non-EU states in Europe: Andorra, San Marino, Montenegro, Macedonia and so on. Of its thirty-four active FTAs, nineteen are with other European states and territories. There are a few more with a handful of ex-colonies. But the big and growing markets of the world are largely ignored. The EU has no trade deals in place with Russia or China, India or Indonesia. It has been talking for years to Brazil and Argentina, but keeps coming up against the fact that these countries want to sell their cheap and delicious meat into Europe. Its talks with Australia have stalled over Italian tomato exports. Its deal with Canada, which looked as though it had been completed, is now being held up because Romania and Bulgaria have dragged it into an unrelated row about visa-free access for their nationals.

EFTA's deals, by contrast, are global. It has either

Fig. 1

THE EU'S FREE TRADE AGREEMENTS

- ■ EU and Customs Union
- ■ European Economic Area
- ▦ Countries with which the EU has a preferential trade agreement in place
- ▨ Countries with which the EU negotiates or has a preferential agreement that is not yet applied
- ⠿ Countries with which the EU is considering opening preferential negotiations
- ░ Countries with which the EU is negotiating a stand-alone investment agreement

Source: European Commission, DG Trade
Map by FreeVectorMaps.com

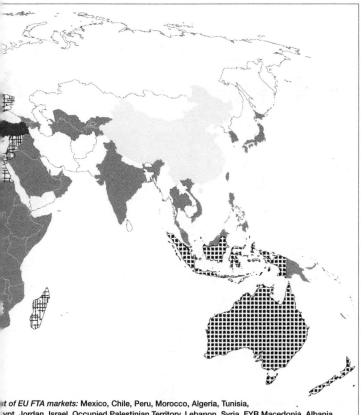

st of EU FTA markets: Mexico, Chile, Peru, Morocco, Algeria, Tunisia,
ypt, Jordan, Israel, Occupied Palestinian Territory, Lebanon, Syria, FYR Macedonia, Albania,
rbia, Montenegro, Bosnia and Herzegovina, Switzerland, Korea, Antigua, Barbuda, Belize,
hamas, Barbados, Dominica, Dominican Repulbic, Grenada, Guyana, Haiti, Jamaica,
Kitts and Nevis, St Lucia, St Vincent and the Grenadines, Suriname, Trinidad and Tobago,
lombia, Honduras, Nicaragua, Panama, Guatemala, Papua New Guinea, South Africa,
adagascar, Mauritius, Seychelles, Zimbabwe, Costa Rica, El Salvador, Fiji, Cameroon,
orgia, Moldova, Ukraine, EU Customs Union (Andorra, Monaco, San Marino,
key), EEA (Norway, Iceland, Liechtenstein).

Fig. 2

EFTA Free Trade Agreements

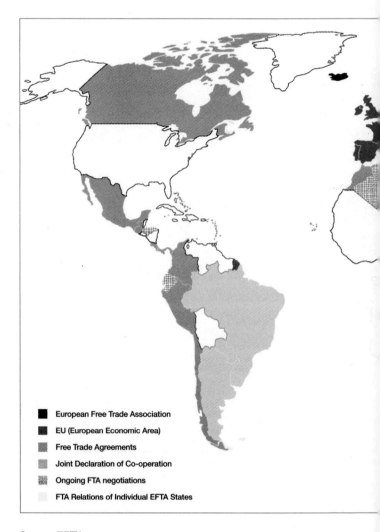

Source: EFTA

agreed, or is actively pursuing, deals with important states in fast-growing regions, especially Asia and the Americas, as the maps above show. Returning to EFTA would simplify and speed these trade deals for the UK – as well as adding impetus to those not yet concluded.

Finally, rejoining EFTA would provide a framework for the UK's future relationship with the EU-27. A regulatory structure exists to maintain free trade between EFTA and the EU, with a small secretariat and a tribunal. While these structures would still leave much to be negotiated, including the tricky issues of financial services rules and migration arrangements, an early indication that Britain would transition from the EU into EFTA with no intervening stage would dispel any doubts about the continuation of free trade.

It might just be possible to solve the European (or British) problem after seventy years of misunderstandings and missed opportunities. Britain's departure from the EU may finally open the possibility of a wider restructuring in Europe, one that would bring benefits both to the countries that want political union and to those that want free trade only. We shouldn't aim at returning to a 1960 arrangement, a Europe (in the phrase of the time) 'at Sixes and Sevens'. Rather, we should be more ambitious: we should use the fact of Brexit to try to secure a pan-continental free market that would bring benefits to all the countries involved. Let us now explore how such a dispensation might be brought about.

4

THE ROAD
NOT TAKEN

I N SEPTEMBER 2015, while David Cameron was
touring the capitals of Europe, feeling out the possibility of a deal, Lord Owen, the former Labour foreign
secretary, proposed a new settlement which, he hoped,
had the potential to satisfy all sides.

In a short book called *Europe Restructured*, he
set out a plan to carve off the EU's economic and
commercial functions from its political functions. The
division would be structural. The institutions that
administered a European free-trade zone would be
answerable to all the countries that participated in
that zone; those which had to do with non-economic

issues, such as foreign policy and criminal justice, would be administered only by those states that had chosen the path of political union.

Lord Owen called the market-only group the 'European Community', and envisaged it covering all EFTA and EU states, as well as Turkey and possibly other European territories. Those states within the European Community which also wanted political integration would form what he called the 'European Union'. The European Union would continue to be responsible for the euro, a common defence policy and so on.

Had the British government taken up the Owen plan, it could have saved itself and the rest of the EU a great deal of trouble. It's worth emphasizing that Lord Owen was at that stage still a Remain supporter. Indeed, he had a better European pedigree than almost any contemporary British politician, having left the Labour Party partly in protest at its switch to an anti-EEC position in 1981.

Lord Owen, in other words, was not just another grandee with an opinion. He was a uniquely qualified foreign-affairs specialist who, after much deliberation and consultation, was recommending an achievable compromise: a set of reforms that would allow him, and other moderates, to support continued EU membership.

Sure enough, his scheme won enthusiastic support from many middle-ground commentators. Here, for example, is the brilliant *Times* columnist Danny Finkelstein, who ended up backing Remain:

Owen argues – surely correctly – that David Cameron's idea of removing ourselves from a commitment to 'ever-closer union' should be a much more ambitious proposal. The prime minister should argue for a community restructured into two parts: the eurozone and the single market. Or to put it another way, the Union and the Community.

These negotiations are the big opportunity for Eurosceptics who want to be in Europe but not run by Europe. It is vital that the prime minister be bold in his proposals and realistic about what the future holds for Britain in an EU dominated by the eurozone and its needs.[27]

It was good advice – advice, moreover, offered by a writer who was as close to David Cameron as any writer can be. Danny Finkelstein wasn't just an old friend to the PM. He wasn't just a peer in receipt of the Conservative whip. He was, it has emerged since the vote, visiting Number 10 every month to prepare

27 *The Times*, 2 September 2015

material for David Cameron's memoirs, which he is now ghost-writing. It is impossible to imagine that Lord Finkelstein didn't offer his old friend in private the same excellent advice that he was offering in public. So why wasn't it taken up?

Not, contrary to widespread belief, because of immovable resistance in the rest of the EU. The all-or-nothing insistence on the *finalité politique* which had held sway in Europe's palaces and chancelleries from the late 1950s to the late 1990s had mellowed. While almost all Eurocrats and most national leaders still favoured some form of political assimilation, they now tempered their ambition with realism. The doctrine that there could be no permanent opt-outs, only temporary derogations, had been largely abandoned.

The key moment had come with the euro crisis, and the realization that the single currency would not survive unless, in defiance of all the rules, the EU found a way to transfer large sums of money to Greece. That was when, as the former German foreign minister Joschka Fischer put it, 'something fundamental to the EU cracked'.

By the time David Cameron announced his intention to seek a different deal, that fissure was widely accepted. No one in Brussels seriously expected, say, Denmark to join the euro, or Ireland to join Schengen.

Although the dream of a federal Europe continued to exert its quasi-spiritual pull on European politicians and functionaries, they had become more relaxed about the geography of the eventual federation.

Even before the British renegotiations had started, the EU had formally accepted – grudgingly, perhaps, but in a spirit of realism – that not every member state was going to interpret the Treaty of Rome's commitment to 'ever-closer union' in the same way.

Among the strongest enthusiasts for that change were, oddly enough, the true believers: Jacques Delors, who had overseen the transformation of the EEC into the EU; Valéry Giscard d'Estaing, author of the European Constitution; and Guy Verhofstadt, the ultra-federalist former Belgian premier, and leader of the Euroliberals, who is now the European Parliament's Brexit negotiator.

Why were these men content to let Britain opt out of political union? Because they understood that Britain's withdrawal into an outer tier, a trade-based association, would make a United States of Europe more feasible. Indeed, they had led calls for such a restructuring. Delors had called for a 'privileged partnership' for the United Kingdom, which he envisaged as continued membership of the European market, bolstered by close intergovernmental collaboration with its neighbours, but removal from the non-economic aspects of the EU. Verhofstadt had proposed much the same thing, calling it 'associate membership'.

Such a deal would, if the polls were to be believed, have satisfied four in five British voters. So, again, why on Earth didn't Downing Street strive to make it happen?

Part of the answer had to do with an understandable miscalculation. When David Cameron announced in January 2013 that there would be a referendum before the end of 2017, he assumed, as did almost everyone else, that there would need to be a new Intergovernmental Conference to legalize the fiscal harmonization necessitated by the euro crisis. At the very least, there would surely have to be a new treaty retrospectively to authorize the bailouts, which had been patently illegal.

The plan was therefore to strike a grand bargain. The United Kingdom would gladly support eurozone member states pursuing deeper integration through the EU if, in return, it was allowed to repatriate substantial powers to Westminster.

But David Cameron – and, in fairness, most of Europe – underestimated the EU's readiness to act outside its own rules. No one in Brussels denied that the bailouts had been unlawful, not just in the sense that there was no basis for them in the treaties, but in the sense that they had been expressly prohibited. Yet, at the same time, no one in Brussels much wanted a new treaty, which would need to be ratified by all twenty-eight national parliaments and, in at least some cases, also by referendum. They were content to act without correct legal authority more or less indefinitely.

From the moment he announced the renegotiation at the imposing headquarters of the business news agency Bloomberg, David Cameron had been clear that there would need to be a new treaty. Without one, there could be no substantial change.

The obstacle he ran up against was not a principled objection to giving Britain a looser deal; it was, rather, a natural reluctance to embark on a time-consuming set of changes. Why, after all, should the rest of the EU undertake the tedious process of summoning a formal Intergovernmental Conference when almost no one believed that Britain might actually vote to leave?

To my knowledge, every British Eurocrat, from our commissioner downwards, continuously reassured colleagues that Brexit was vanishingly unlikely. Indeed, Jean-Claude Juncker rather indiscreetly blurted out that David Cameron had privately assured him of his intention to use the referendum 'to dock Britain permanently in the EU'.[28]

28 *Süddeutsche Zeitung*, 1 June 2016

So there was, on one level, a simple tactical failure on the part of British negotiators. They never seriously communicated that a Leave vote was a viable possibility – largely because they never believed it themselves. They therefore failed to secure even the minimalist changes that they had publicly promised, including a new treaty.

This tactical error was compounded by a strategic one. British negotiators pushed for the wrong things. Instead of reaching out to Eurosceptics, and finding out what motivated them, they appear to have decided at the outset, more or less on a hunch, that the only important issues were migration and benefits.

In fact, the polling data, then as now, showed that sovereignty was by far the larger concern for potential Leave voters. Yet, like so many supporters of the EU, the PM and chancellor seem to have come to believe in the caricature of the bigoted Eurosceptic. Instead of pushing for a general recovery of non-market-related powers, they put all their negotiating eggs into the immigration and welfare baskets.

This was not only a less significant goal for most (not all) Eurosceptics; it was also, paradoxically, harder to deliver. No one in Brussels really minded whether the UK remained in, say, the EU's common diplomatic corps (the EEAS) or its prosecuting magistracy (Eurojust).

It would have been relatively simple, administratively, to withdraw from various non-market institutions and programmes; doing so would not have impinged on the interests of the other twenty-seven states.

Free movement, by contrast, was always going to be a thornier question. Some member nations had large expatriate communities in the UK (with the right to vote in their countries of origin). Others thought of free movement as a single-market issue, and therefore a core rather than a peripheral function of the EU. Angela Merkel, who had grown up in the GDR, saw free movement as an important human right.

David Cameron therefore struggled to secure any concessions in the fields he saw as central; and he had barely sought concessions in other areas.

As we saw in the last chapter, the main concern for Eurosceptic campaigners, right from the start, had been avoiding a political union with the other countries, a United States of Europe. David Cameron gained no ground in this field whatever, and seems hardly to have tried. He came back with a declaration to the effect that not all member states had to interpret 'ever-closer union' in the same way – which was simply a reiteration of a previous EU communiqué.

That pledge was meaningless. We know what polit-ical union means to Euro-integrationists. The scheme has been set out by Jacques Delors and Angela Merkel and other federalists a thousand times. The European Commission becomes the EU's executive government, the Parliament becomes its federal legislature, the Council of Ministers becomes its Senate or Upper Chamber and the ECJ becomes its Supreme Court. As long as the United Kingdom remained part of all those institutions, and as long as it accepted the supremacy of EU over national law, no declaration would slow its absorption into a united Europe.

In fairness, most Remainers knew this, which is why so little was made of the declaration during the referendum.

How can I say with confidence that the British government failed to ask for the right things? We know that it was never publicly committed to the kind of restructuring that David Owen had proposed or, indeed, to any significant repatriations of power: that is a matter of record. But might its public position have been drawn up on the basis of what was privately thought to be achievable? Might British officials have made some early informal approaches, seeking a more significant deal? Might they have withdrawn because these probes ran up against adamantine resistance in Brussels? Might it be, in other words, that, despite what Messrs Delors and Giscard and Verhofstadt were saying, the EU was unwilling to let Britain have a looser deal?

No. I know for a fact that ministers never sought such an outcome. Shortly after David Cameron had made his Bloomberg speech, I spoke to the Europe minister, David Lidington, a man who combines towering integrity (he is, among other things, a lay preacher) with towering intelligence (he captained the all-time University Challenge champion team). I told him that the speech had gone down very well in the EFTA countries, and offered to put him in touch with some of the politicians there who were already thinking in terms of looking for a form of associate status that their countries might enjoy alongside the UK.

David was, as he invariably is, affable, honest and direct: 'That's not the direction the government wants to go,' he said, explaining that the goal was an improvement of our existing membership terms, not wholly different terms.

Later, following the UKIP surge in the 2014 European election, and the subsequent defections of my friends Douglas Carswell and Mark Reckless to UKIP, I tried again.

I arranged to see David Cameron at Number 10, and found him, too, affable, honest and direct. I began by telling him that I wanted his renegotiation to succeed. To hope for a failure simply so that the subsequent referendum would be more likely to end in a Leave vote would, I suggested, be downright unpatriotic. We Eurosceptics, for the most part, saw leaving the EU, not as an end in itself, but as a means to an end, that end being a freer and more prosperous Britain. If he could deliver the same end by securing a fundamental restructuring in Europe, leaving us inside the common market but outside the political union, that'd do for most of us.

The PM listened politely, asked one or two intelligent questions and then said something like this: 'You've always had a clear position on the EU, and I respect that. It's a perfectly legitimate view, but it happens not to be my view. I think our relationship with the EU needs to change, but I've never believed that we should just have a kind of free-trade-plus deal. If that's what you want, fine. You should work to get a Conservative victory in May, then we'll have our In–Out referendum and you can campaign to leave.'

Very well, I said, I will. And I did.

I don't tell that story in any carping spirit. In all the time that I dealt with him as party leader, I found David Cameron to be purposeful, pleasant and professional. I admired him as a politician, though I sensed my admiration wasn't reciprocated. Certainly,

I have no complaints about his record on the EU. He promised a referendum and he delivered. But for him, we wouldn't now be looking at the prospect of a global future.

No, I mention that conversation to make an important point about Britain's present options. We now have the chance to secure a deal that is roughly along the lines that David Owen proposed, but that David Cameron chose not to pursue.

Britain's relationship with the EU has been cursed by unlucky timing. We have been Rhett and Scarlett; or, if you prefer, Romeo and Juliet, or Pyramus and Thisbe. At first, the insistence in Brussels that political union was the end, and a customs union the means, made British participation impossible. But when, in the early 1990s, the possibility was floated of a European Economic Space that might extend to non-EU states, British policymakers wanted none of it. John Major and Douglas Hurd used to speak with a shudder of a 'two-tier Europe' in which Britain might find itself 'relegated' to the outer tier.

Throughout the Blair years, instead of working to make a looser form of membership viable, Britain pursued the vain dream of leading in Europe. Tony Blair desperately wanted to join the euro and, until his final day in office, longed to be president of the EU.

David Cameron never seriously contemplated any form of associate status. He placed immense value on his seat at the table during deliberations. There is no dishonour in that impulse: it's only human to confuse your presence with the national interest. The trouble is that this led him to seek only such changes as were commensurate with full British membership.

Might he have got a looser deal? Without question. Plenty of people urged David Cameron to hold out for significant concessions and call the referendum in 2017, including his chief whip and his planet-brained election strategist, Lynton Crosby. But the PM was in no mood to wait. Perhaps he was nervous about the impact of the continuing migratory flow into Europe. Perhaps he didn't want half of his second term to be consumed with the referendum preparations. Perhaps (and who can blame him after his unexpected victory in the general election?) he was overconfident.

Whatever his motives, David Cameron decided to cut and run, going for the earliest possible referendum on any terms he could get. His fellow heads of government, seeing almost no prospect of a British Leave vote, interpreted their role as an essentially theatrical one. They were happy to make it look as though there had been a row, as though something significant had been asked for and granted; but they saw no reason to reopen the treaties. Britain was going to stay, the issue would be put to bed, integration could continue.

Plainly, the situation has now been transformed. The option of Britain remaining in the EU on essentially unchanged terms has gone. But what of the idea of a trade-only relationship? And what of using the opportunity of Brexit to rationalize the higgledy-piggledy arrangements which the EU has with those nineteen other European states and territories, from Iceland and the Faroe Islands to Turkey and Georgia? Might it now be time to apply a version of the Owen plan?

It hardly needs saying that the details are vital. Delineating the border between market and non-market issues is far from straightforward. The Brussels institutions have long been in the habit of defining any contentious proposal as a single-market measure, so as to make it subject to majority voting. For example, because the UK had opted out of the harmonization of employment laws in 1991, the EU was legally not to subject it to the forty-eight-hour week that the other eleven states had had to adopt. Its solution? To propose precisely the same directive as a 'health-and-safety' measure, thereby making it subject to majority voting and allowing the other states to impose it on Britain. What made that episode especially farcical is that the directive in question allowed employees to work for more than forty-eight hours *provided they were paid overtime*. Whatever else it was, it was plainly not a health-and-safety measure.

The EU has taken the same approach with other legislation that does not command unanimous support. For example, most of its environmental laws, including the entire carbon-trading scheme, have been defined as single-market measures.

Any new arrangement would need to avoid the centralizing bias of the European Commission and the judicial activism of the ECJ. The institutions that oversaw the pan-European market would need to be separate from the EU's organs. Some precedent exists in the way that EFTA regulates its relationship with the EU. The EFTA Surveillance Authority and the EFTA Court shadow their EU counterparts in Brussels and Luxembourg, although operating outside EU jurisdiction. It's true that some EFTA commentators believe that these institutions are too ready simply to transpose EU rulings. Still, there is a difference between a four-member EFTA made up only of small states and a twenty-member European Community that included Britain and Turkey.

Then there is the whole question of free movement. We have already seen that it is possible to be in the European market while having some opt-outs. Liechtenstein does so, and Switzerland would almost certainly have secured a similar deal had its talks not been overtaken by the British referendum. Again, there will need to be negotiations, but it is at least possible to envisage a deal that preserved the right of citizens to take up job offers, while divorcing that entitlement from the right of settlement. Taking away the right to come to another EU state without an existing job and removing in-work benefits for an initial period of four or five years would substantially cut numbers, while allowing employers to find the labour they needed. It may be that, in order to reassure the public, such measures would be combined with a cap on numbers though, in reality, these would be almost certain to fall as a result of the other changes.

Finally, and most importantly, there is the question of obeying common standards – the distinction, in other words, between *access to* and *membership of* the single market.

Many commentators insist on seeing this question as being bound up with that of migration. They imagine a trade-off between single-market membership (supposedly a good thing) and the free movement of people (supposedly a bad thing). In fact, the two issues do not need to be linked. The argument against single-market membership is not that it's too high a price to pay for immigration; it's that it restricts economic growth.

Our starting point, when it comes to setting technical standards or, indeed, recognizing qualifications, should be reciprocity rather than harmonization. If our aim to create a broader, pan-continental market whose purpose is to maximize prosperity rather than to encourage political integration (that latter task now being carried out separately, among the countries that have opted for full EU membership), then we will need a very different attitude to regulation.

First, we will need to distinguish between goods and services that are traded across borders and those – the vast majority in the case of Britain, as of other large economies – that are not. This is a key difference between the EU and, say, NAFTA or ASEAN. Classical free-trade areas tend not to concern themselves with behind-border issues in the way that the EU does.

While it makes sense to agree common rules for commodities that are traded internationally, there is no advantage in imposing these rules on firms – generally smaller and medium-sized enterprises – that do most of their business locally. Let small firms worry about European regulations only when they want to export.

Britain should use withdrawal from the EU as an opportunity to prune its regulations and set a precedent for easier global trade. Consider, to take an example more or less at random, the pharmaceuticals industry. Outside the EU, Britain will presumably have a regulator which determines what drugs may be sold. The starting point for that regulator ought to be that any product approved by the FDA for the United States or by the EMA for the EU, or by equivalent regulators in Canada, Australia or other comparable countries, can be legally bought and sold in Britain. Our presumption should be in favour of recognizing the standards of other countries unless someone can show an overwhelming reason not to.

Britain, in conclusion, should seek, outside the EU, to draw other non-members into a lightly regulated market that would enjoy complete free trade with the EU without the extraneous ties. Whether this is done by expanding EFTA or, in time, by creating a wholly new structure, of the kind proposed by Lord Owen, matters less than the substance, namely being in a common market rather than in a political union.

I say 'common market' rather than 'single market'. Britain should sign up to common rules for the goods and services it wants to buy from or sell to its European allies. It should not have to apply those rules to its entire domestic economy. In other words, any new arrangement would need to be based, as EFTA is, on mutual recognition rather than on standardization.

Two questions arise. First, why should the EU twenty-seven agree to such a proposition? Second, even if they agreed in general terms, why should they grant access to British financial-services exports?

The answer to the first question would be obvious but for the fraught atmosphere that lingers after the referendum. Countries don't trade with one another out of kindness. Indeed, countries don't really trade with other countries at all – businesses trade with businesses.

Free commerce is always – *always* – beneficial to both parties. Otherwise it wouldn't happen. An extension of trade within and beyond the European continent will bring advantages to every country involved.

What's in it for the EU twenty-seven? Greater wealth. Free trade with Britain or Ukraine or Turkey is plainly preferable to restricted trade. And rationalizing the cat's-cradle of different arrangements with the Isle of Man and Macedonia and Switzerland and the rest would be both productive of freer trade and administratively cheaper.

The EU has already called for such rationalization. In 2012, it began looking at ways to draw San

Marino, Andorra, Monaco and the other microstates into some sort of EFTA or EEA arrangement for the sake of administrative simplicity. The non-EU Faroe Islands, too, have expressed an interest in joining EFTA, although there is a constitutional complexity there in that they are under Danish suzerainty, and so can't sit as a sovereign entity in international bodies.

Obviously, being outside the EU core, the UK and others would have no say over what standards the core states set among themselves; but nor would they have to apply those standards except when selling across borders. There might be occasions when, for the sake of economies of scale, it suited Britain to adopt the same standards as the EU. Switzerland often shadows EU regulation when the size of its European markets make that a sensible move. Equally, there will be many occasions when both Britain and the EU are following the same global rules.

On these occasions, incidentally, Britain will be in a far stronger position to influence the legislation as an independent state than it is now as an EU member. Regulations are increasingly set at a planetary rather than a continental level. On everything from food-safety standards to banking rules, the EU and other countries are, in effect, implementing standards made by global bodies (food standards and banking rules, for example, are largely governed by the UN's *codex alimentarius* and the Basle III regulations respectively). At present, when those standards are set, the UK is represented by one twenty-eighth of a European commissioner. After independence, it will resume its own seat at the table alongside the US, Norway, New Zealand, the EU and the rest.

How will the broader European free-trade area interact with the remaining EU, which will presumably still be a customs union? Can a customs union sit comfortably as a sub-group within a larger free-trade area? For example, if the UK follows Switzerland and signs a free-trade agreement with China, why shouldn't Chinese firms sell into the UK and then move their goods, tariff-free, straight into the EU?

This is not a new dilemma. Indeed, it applies all over the world, and the World Trade Organization (WTO) has worked out how to resolve it. Goods these days are generally shipped in bulk, so tracing whether a consignment originated in China is not a problem. The problem, potentially, would arise if China exported goods to the UK and had them tweaked in some tiny way so as to be categorized as a British product for the purpose of re-export to the EU.

The way the WTO deals with this problem is through what are known as 'rules of origin': technical schedules that, in effect, define how much of any given product has to be made in a country for the product to be labelled as coming from that country. If jam is made and put into jars in, say, Canada, and the jars are then exported to Switzerland where labels are added to them, the jam still counts as Canadian for the purpose of exports. WTO rules even specify the proportion of fruit content that would need to come from Switzerland before the jam became Swiss.

Britain would find itself, if it were to leave the EU and join EFTA, or some expanded form of it, in the same position as Switzerland today. In theory, there could be customs checks now between Switzerland and the EU. In practice, the Swiss border to the EU is barely noticeable – except that non-Swiss cars are required to purchase a disc that allows them to use Swiss highways, in recognition of the fact that they have paid no road tax. Of course, Swiss customs officers, or immigration officers, might act on a tip-off and search a specific vehicle. In practical terms, though, the frontier is open and millions of EU nationals cross it every month, without passport checks, to work in the Helvetic Confederation.

Since Britain's points of entry are airports or seaports (with the exception of Ireland, which we shall look at later), travellers would notice no difference. There would be red and green lanes as now, allowing for the possibility of searches. As regards sea-borne freight, there are tariff-free areas in most large commercial ports in which goods can be landed and reshipped without formally entering the country. The processing is now done by computer though, again, the possibility of spot checks exists.

In truth, though, no one expects tariffs or other impediments to the free movement of goods. Britain and the EU are beginning from a position of zero tariffs and quotas with each other, and no serious politician on either side is proposing to impose new ones. Not even the most enthusiastic Remain campaigners are still trying, now that the referendum is over, to raise that prospect.

But what about services? Here, the issue is a different one. The barriers to free commerce don't take the form of duties, but of protectionist regulations. Rules can be drawn up in such a way as to exclude foreign competition and privilege some local vested interest – to the detriment of local consumers, to be sure, but that doesn't stop it happening.

Britain is a major exporter of services. Is it conceivable that the rest of the EU, while cheerfully agreeing to free trade in goods (where Britain runs a large trade deficit with the other twenty-seven), will seek to regulate services in a way designed to exclude British competition?

Such a thing is possible. Indeed, it would be possible whether or not Britain remained in the EU. We often read of the risk of Britain being 'excluded' from 'the single market in services'. But no such market exists. During my years as an MEP, I have come across many examples of services protectionism, from British ski instructors banned from working in France to British language teachers unable to ply their trade in Italy.

We need, in any case, to distinguish between a free-trade agreement and actual free trade. Britain is, as we keep being told, a big exporter of financial services, many of which are indeed sold in other EU states. If you define financial services at their widest, including pensions and insurance, the rest of the EU took 33 per cent of our total exports in 2014, according to the Office for National Statistics. (It's worth noting, *en passant*, that that figure is in decline, as are all our exports to the EU: in 2005, the EU was taking 39 per cent of our financial-services exports, defined in that same broad way.)

But consider this: in 2014, the United States alone was taking 31 per cent of our financial-services exports. Yet there is absolutely no free-trade deal between Britain and the United States – because there is no trade deal between the EU and the United States. The lack of a formal treaty has not prevented the United States from being by far Britain's single best export market for financial services.

To repeat, trade is not an act of generosity. 'It is not from the benevolence of the butcher, the brewer or the baker that we expect our dinner, but from their regard to their own interest,' wrote Adam Smith. Nor is it from the benevolence of the banker that we expect our mortgage. As workers in financial services around Europe have repeatedly pointed out, the success of the City of London does not only benefit the United Kingdom; it offers opportunities to everyone who trades there.

Britain should seek free trade in services with the EU, as with the rest of the world. But it should not do so at the price of burdening London (to say nothing of Edinburgh and our other financial-services centres) with rules that place Britain at a competitive disadvantage vis-à-vis non-EU financial centres.

This is not a hypothetical argument. Since the credit crunch, there has been a change in the focus of EU financial regulation. Whereas until 2009 it could be argued that most Brussels directives tended to be liberalizing, and therefore to require more rule changes in Continental countries than in the UK, the mood altered after the collapse of Lehman. Capitalism in general, and London in particular, were blamed for the crisis. Numerous regulations were imposed on Britain, despite the resistance of both the financial-services industry and the government. On four occasions, the government was driven to the extreme step of challenging EU financial regulations in court. It lost three of the four cases, succeeding only in fighting off an attempt to ban trading in euro-denominated securities in London – though, frankly, it is hard to see how such a ban could be enforced once Britain is no longer in the EU.

Many of the EU's regulations imposed costs which far outweighed any notional advantages in easier trade – though, naturally, the industry was readier to make that argument before assimilating those costs than it is now. The Alternative Investment Fund Managers Directive, for example, imposed massive regulatory inconvenience on UK equity funds. The Solvency II rules hurt UK insurance firms, prompting Prudential to announce that it might move to Asia in consequence. The short-selling ban was squarely aimed at the City. And more is in the pipeline, starting with the potentially ruinous Financial Transactions Tax.

The question for Britain, and more especially for the City, is where to make the trade-off. How much inconvenient regulation should we be prepared to assimilate for the sake of being able to continue to sell into the EU on existing terms? After all, it's not Europe that is in competition with London. Our rivals are further afield: New York, Singapore, Shanghai.

So far, London has performed extraordinarily well in that global race. It recently overtook Singapore to become the largest trading centre for renminbi outside China. It is arguably the world capital of Islamic banking, and leads the FinTech revolution. London has been able to hold that position by combining a trusted legal system and a light regulatory regime with unparalleled support services. Adopting burdensome regulation for the sake of uniformity with the EU would disadvantage London relative to its non-EU competitors.

Consider what might be the effect on this global race of, say, the EU's cap on bonuses. Even in the understandable anger that followed the financial crash, it never made much sense to target the one part of a banker's package that is performance-related. Instead of tackling rewards for failure, we were bizarrely decoupling remuneration from results. Sure enough, many EU firms have responded to the limit by whacking up salaries in compensation.

Now ask this question: if you were a hungry and clever young financier, with big dreams and boundless energy, where would you rather make your career? In a city where relative mediocrities were cushioned by high salaries, but the rewards for exceptional outcomes were limited by statute – or in one of the Asian financial centres that applauded risk-taking?

Concerns were raised, both during the referendum campaign and after the vote, about the right of City institutions to 'passport' their services across the EU. Passporting was the flip side of the intrusive regulatory structure introduced in 2013 by the AIFMD and the creation of various EU supervisory bodies. It allows financial-services operators based in one member state to operate in the other twenty-seven.

Yet almost every EU legal act that provides for passporting also provides for 'equivalence'. Equivalence means that a firm based outside the EU can also trade freely across the EU provided its financial regulation is deemed to be equivalent, in its scope, purpose and reliability to that found within the EU.

Which states are deemed to pass muster? In July 2016, the EU's regulator recommended that passporting be extended to firms regulated in Australia, Canada, the Cayman Islands, Guernsey, Hong Kong, Japan, Jersey, Switzerland and the United States. Now remember that on the day Brexit takes effect, Britain won't just have *equivalent* regulation to the EU; it will have *identical* regulation. The idea that Japan might enjoy passporting rights but not the UK is risible.

The fact that this fear is being raised at all suggests that some of the London-based megabanks are being swayed by the interests of their Brussels-based lobbyists rather than those of their shareholders. Obviously, the government relations staff in these giant institutions have a vested interest in remaining as closely involved as possible in EU regulatory structures: that is where their expertise lies. But free trade based on regulatory equivalence is, almost by definition, preferable to regulation by the EU. It allows each sector – indeed, each firm – to decide whether its EU market is so significant that it makes sense to adopt otherwise undesirable rules for the sake of continued automatic access. Instead of having that choice imposed on them, they can act according to their own interests, opening a small office abroad if the gains outweigh the costs.

What if, over time, the EU goes in a much more protectionist direction? What if it imposes barriers and rules that cause it to diverge from London and other competitive financial centres to the extent that, in some sectors, regulatory equivalence no longer applies?

We can't wholly discount the possibility, at least not in the long term. There are populist and anti-market tendencies in several EU states, from France's Front National to Greece's Syriza. If they decide to make life harder for financial services providers, they will cause themselves great harm and, in the process, do some incidental damage to the UK, which naturally has an immediate interest in the prosperity of its neighbours. But, as long as we are outside the EU, the damage inflicted by Euro-corporatism and protectionism will be collateral rather than direct. We can't ultimately stop the EU cutting itself off from world financial markets; but at least we will be free to stand aside if it does so.

To summarize, then, we should use the opportunity of Brexit to create a different form of European architecture – one in which the nineteen European states and territories that currently trade freely with the EU can join with it and Britain to create a pan-continental market, lightly regulated, and based on the principle of mutual product recognition rather than harmonization. The EU twenty-seven would form an inner core within that market. I write 'the EU twenty-seven', though it is, of course, perfectly feasible that other EU states might prefer a British-type status to membership of the inner core. Provision should be made for such states to follow Britain, should they wish, with minimum disruption.

One way to stimulate such a reorganization would be for the UK to rejoin EFTA. But EFTA should not be the limit of our ambition. Our goal should be to spread European free trade as widely as possible, without regard for politics or geography. Once we detach the question of free trade in goods and services from that of political integration, it becomes much more feasible to extend the market to any country that expresses an interest in joining – Morocco, Tunisia, Israel, Ukraine.

We should seek to ensure that mutual recognition continues to apply to services. We should be prepared to align our regulations with those of other countries where the benefits of easier market penetration outweigh the compliance costs; but we should not accept supranational regulation. We must retain the freedom to step aside when the regulatory price becomes too high.

At the same time, we should seek to stimulate a revival of global trade liberalization by cutting our tariffs and other trade barriers – a subject to which we shall come presently. We should seek, too, to reform our domestic approach to regulation, so that there is a presumption in favour of non-intervention – of which, again, more in a moment.

The vision, though, is clear enough: here is our chance to create a free-trading, deregulated, off-shore Britain – an entrepôt trading with the EU and the rest of the world, working for the reciprocal dismantling of tariff and non-tariff barriers wherever possible, but being prepared to reduce its own barriers unilaterally if necessary. The UK should retain the closest links with its EU allies commensurate with full sovereignty, including the military commitment of NATO, open markets through EFTA or an EFTA-type arrangement and formalized intergovernmental co-operation. At the same time, it should strengthen its political and economic ties to non-EU states.

That, at any rate, should be our goal. But how, in the strained post-referendum atmosphere, are we to secure it? How can we convince our EU allies that leaving the EU, far from being an unfriendly act, can lead to an improved relationship? How, in short, do we ensure an amicable divorce?

5

ARTICLE 50 AND ALL THAT

THE LAST CHAPTER set out a scheme for a general restructuring of Europe, one which would draw a distinction between a broader association of states, concerned mainly with free trade, and an inner core which also maintained a single currency, a common defence force and so on.

Such a restructuring should be Britain's goal in the negotiations, but we also need a back-up plan. While the removal of certain states from supranational institutions is certainly achievable – indeed, influential voices in Brussels are already advancing the idea – nothing in life is certain. We should prepare for the possibility, however unlikely, that some EU member governments or Brussels institutions will not act from self-interest, but from spite. Divorce proceedings are not always guided by logic and, though there is a difference between the breakdown of a marriage and a set of negotiations carried out by professional diplomats, it is at least conceivable that some in the EU will want to see the Brexit process as a zero-sum game.

As we look at the technicalities of the exit process, therefore, we should plan for two scenarios: one in which the talks are cordial and productive, based around the desire to maximize benefits to both sides; and one in which Brussels seeks difficult exit terms, so as to discourage any other state from following Britain.

So far, the signs point to the former scenario. In the run-up to Britain's referendum, the German government suggested that Brexit would mean it being treated like any third country. Now, the German Europe minister, Michael Roth, says: 'Given Britain's size, significance and long membership of the European Union, there will probably be a special status which only bears limited comparison to that of countries that have never belonged to the European Union. I want relations between the European Union and Britain to be as close as possible.'[29]

'I can't imagine a situation where we have more barriers on trade,' says Geert Bourgeois, prime minister

29 Reuters, 16 August 2016

of Flanders. 'It is in our mutual interest to find a solution, and the majority of the EU now agrees that anything other than a soft Brexit would have a huge cost.'[30]

Other governments have made similar noises, talking of the need to preserve close relations with the United Kingdom and to maximize the mutual prosperity that comes from cross-Channel trade.

Would the Brussels institutions contemplate the sort of deal sketched out in Chapter Four – a two-tier Europe in which Britain and other states could remain in a common market, while standing aside from supranational rules?

As a matter of fact, this scheme is seen by many Eurocrats, not as a minimally acceptable compromise, but as their preferred outcome.

On 29 August 2016, the Bruegel Institute in Brussels published its considered response to the UK referendum, entitled 'Europe after Brexit'. Launched by Jacques Chirac and Gerhard Schröder, with the former EU Commissioner Mario Monti as its first chairman, Bruegel is the closest thing to an official EU think tank. Uniquely, it is funded by EU governments, giving it a semi-formal status.

Bruegel's starting point is that, while Britain has

30 *Daily Telegraph*, 23 August 2016

voted to recover sovereignty, including sovereignty in migration policy, that goal ought not to be incompatible with a continuing close relationship based on a common market:

> Neither the EU nor the UK have an interest in a divorce that diminishes their influence as the balance of economic power shifts away from the North-Atlantic world. We propose a new form of collaboration, a continental partnership. The UK will want to have some control over labour mobility, as well as leaving behind the EU's supranational decision-making. The proposed continental partnership would consist in participating in goods, services, capital mobility and some temporary labour mobility as well as in a new system of inter-governmental decision-making and enforcement of common rules to protect the homogeneity of the deeply integrated market.

The Bruegel paper sets out mechanisms for Britain to remain in a common market, and with a formal role in the formulation of common standards. However, being outside the supranational structures, it would not be able to block the EU from adopting such standards – though, obviously, it could then choose not to apply them except when selling into the EU. Critically, the authors see this deal as a way to regularize the EU's relations with its neighbours on all sides.

> This results in a Europe with an inner circle, the EU, with deep and political integration, and an outer circle with less integration. Over the long-run this could also serve as a vision for structuring relations with Turkey, Ukraine and other countries.

Obviously, what matters here is the detail. Bruegel foresees Britain continuing to pay something into the EU budget, albeit less than now; and, while Britain should of course pay its share of any joint programmes and institutions, it should not be in the business of, for example, making transfer payments to EU countries with lower GDP than its own. British development aid should be targeted at the neediest places in the world, the places where it can make the most difference.

The free-movement question matters, too. Bruegel envisages Britain opting out of this principle, albeit retaining 'some temporary labour mobility'.

There is a difference, too, between having a separate structure invigilating the common market, as David Owen proposes (see p. 110), and having a consultative role (combined with an eventual opt-out) in the existing EU institutions.

Finally, the Bruegel proposal is for Britain to stay inside the EU's common tariffs, which is plainly not going to happen: even many Remainers now concede that freer trade with non-EU states is one of the clear advantages of withdrawal.

Still the positions are not impossibly distant. With goodwill, an acceptable compromise can surely be found during the negotiations.

That said, no one should enter negotiations without a fallback position. Britain must not put itself in the position that Syriza-led Greece was in, when it demanded better bail out terms from Brussels without any contingency plan to leave the euro if it failed to get them. Britain must, in other words, prepare for the scenario, however unlikely, that no trade deal can be agreed with the EU before the disengagement talks are concluded. That means having trade deals with third countries pre-negotiated and ready to enter into force the moment Brexit takes legal effect.

Before we look at those trade deals, let us consider the mechanics of withdrawal. A great deal has been written about Article 50. Its author, the former Italian prime minister, Giuliano Amato, tells us that it was never intended to be activated, and the general consensus is that it has been expressly designed to tilt the balance of advantage against the departing state.

In fact, Article 50 provides a sensible mechanism for a withdrawal to be concluded within the law and without the process being endlessly strung out. It is, in reality, the simplest and most credible way to effect an orderly secession.

It's true that Britain could unilaterally repeal the 1972 European Communities Act, inform its partners that it was walking out and leave the international courts to sort out any residual fees, asset divisions and so on. As a matter of internal constitutional procedure, this is feasible. But it cannot be reconciled with the United Kingdom's commitment to international law, nor with the fact that, in any scenario, the EU states will remain important allies. Britain is bound by Article 60 of the Vienna Convention, which provides for sanctions against states which unilaterally breach treaties. Having entered the EU by treaty, we ought to leave by treaty, with the agreement and, as we hope, the amity of our neighbours.

That, then, leaves only two options: to negotiate a withdrawal treaty, akin to an accession treaty but in reverse; or to trigger Article 50 (the short clauses of this much-referenced article appear in the appendix – see p. 295).

Using Article 50 has two obvious advantages over negotiating a new withdrawal treaty.

First, it provides for a time limit. If the talks are not concluded within two years, the withdrawing state simply leaves, unless an extension is unanimously agreed. Many commentators, for some reason, see this as disadvantageous to Britain, but the alternative would be to seek a treaty which would need to be ratified by all twenty-seven national parliaments. Unlike Article 50, this really might involve (to borrow a favourite Remainer phrase) 'years of uncertainty'. Even with the best will in the world, ratification by all twenty-seven national parliaments would probably take years. And, in the event of a loss of goodwill, the EU twenty-seven would hold all the cards. They could string the process of withdrawal out almost indefinitely, requiring the UK to adopt all EU legislation in the meantime and to pay its full budget contributions.

Second, Article 50 provides for withdrawal to be ratified through qualified majority voting rather than by unanimity. In other words, if one or two countries opposed the deal – either because they wanted a more punitive approach or, more likely, because they were linking it to some unrelated demands of their own – the deal would fall. Invoking Article 50 means that Britain does not need to get every single one of the other twenty-seven EU states to ratify its departure terms.

There is a certain amount of tussling over precisely what may be discussed before Article 50 is formally invoked – something that Theresa May has said will happen before the end of March 2017. Both sides are, as it were, making high opening bids. Some Eurocrats are suggesting that they won't begin trade talks with the UK until withdrawal has been completed. The exit talks, they say, should be narrowly concerned with such issues as who pays the pensions of British Eurocrats. Only when all that has been agreed, they intimate, will discussions turn to our future relationship. The UK has naturally responded to such talk by letting it be known that, in that case, it is in no hurry, and is quite prepared to focus on trade talks with non-EU states until the EU comes round.

In reality, there is likely to be a compromise, whereby the UK's future relationship with the EU is negotiated in tandem with its departure terms. Some informal discussions will explore whether both sides are interested in, for example, the two-tier Europe arrangement sketched out above. There will also presumably be talks with EFTA countries, and possibly other non-EU states, about whether they are interested in broadening the parameters of the talks to include a general reordering of European institutions. Once the boundaries of the negotiations are clear, Article 50 will be triggered and talks can begin in earnest.

From a British point of view, though, the vital thing is to have our fallback in place. This means that we need to advance as far as possible in our trade talks with non-EU states, including EFTA states, so that if no deal is in place by the time the two years come to an end, we are able to transition neatly from one set of trade relations to another.

In theory, we cannot enter into formal trade talks with a third country as long as we are bound by the EU's Common Commercial Policy. In practice, international law does not distinguish between informal pre-talks and official negotiations.

Talks with our non-EU allies should therefore be our first task and, so far, ministers do indeed seem to be prioritizing them. The early signs are encouraging. Many of the world's largest economies, including China, India and the Mercosur states (Argentina, Brazil, Paraguay, Uruguay, Venezuela) have declared their readiness to negotiate commercial accords with a post-EU Britain. At the time of writing, twenty-six non-EU countries have signalled their keenness to sign deals.

In pursuing trade talks, British negotiators should distinguish among three categories of states: first, there are the twenty-seven other EU members; second, there are the thirty-four states and territories with which Britain currently has free-trade agreements by virtue of the fact that *they* have free-trade agreements with the EU (these include the four EFTA states); third, there are the remaining 103 members of the World Trade Organization. It is possible that, before the exit talks are complete, some of these 103 states may conclude their own trade negotiations with the EU and move into the second category.

Britain's initial focus should be on the nations in categories two and three, which collectively take 56 per cent (and growing) of our combined goods and services exports. Talks with the EU twenty-seven might be swift and amicable – the early signs are, as I say, positive – but we cannot let those talks take precedence over our negotiations with the rest of the world.

Let's begin with the thirty-four states which already have trade deals with the EU. As we have seen, most of these states are in Europe and its immediate vicinity, but there are some important overseas markets, too, including South Korea, Mexico and South Africa. In these cases, it should be a remarkably straightforward process simply to retain the content of our existing trade deals. All that would change, from the point of view of the third country, is that it would now be dealing with the British government rather than with the European Commission on behalf of the British government. There is no need, at least initially, to get into substantive negotiations with these states. Our starting point should be that we would carry on as now.

It is conceivable, of course, that one or more of these countries might not want to continue trading freely with Britain, although that seems vanishingly unlikely. Trade talks can sometimes be slow to conclude, usually because of a vested interest in one of the states that resents foreign competition. Once they are up and running, however, their benefits become clear. Indeed, the likely pressure is for these deals to become more liberal, ending some of the quotas and restrictions that the EU insisted on, above all in the fields of agriculture and textiles. And, in the years ahead, British negotiators should indeed look at whether it is possible to extend these deals further. For now, though, we should simply keep them in place.

There is plenty of precedent in international law for rolling over international treaties. When states break apart – as when Serbia and Montenegro or the Czech Republic and Slovakia ended their joint sovereignties – trade treaties are assumed to continue to apply to both successor states unless and until someone proposes modification or repeal. In the case of the United Kingdom, we would not be a new state, but an existing state reclaiming sovereignty in trading matters, so the procedure should be even easier.

An important sub-category of these thirty-four states are the four countries that make up EFTA. I explained in Chapter Three why Britain should not follow Norway, Iceland or Liechtenstein into the EEA. Our goal, rather, should be to negotiate an entirely new deal with the EU which all these countries might regard as preferable to their present terms. Still, it may be that pure EFTA membership without the EEA obligations, *à la Suisse*, is a step toward securing that objective.

I don't want to get too bogged down in technicalities. If the goal is to have a deal with the EU that provides for the free circulation of goods and services on the basis of national sovereignty, EFTA is one route to that end, but not the only one. We might want to make use of the EFTA machinery and extend it to other interested countries; or we might prefer to create new institutions.

I have already mentioned the potential advantages of rejoining EFTA: it would short-cut some trade negotiations; it would save us from having to reinvent the wheel when it came to our talks with the EU; and, if it were known early in the talks process that

Britain would join EFTA the day it left the EU, any doubts about Britain's free-trade orientation would be dispelled. Equally, there may be better ways to secure those objectives. But we shouldn't rule out EFTA simply because we can't be bothered to distinguish between the Norwegian and Swiss models. EEA membership, while still preferable to EU membership, comes with some costs; with pure EFTA membership, those costs are much lower.

The greatest opportunities for Britain, though, are to be found across the oceans in those states with which the EU has no trade deals. Global free trade was mentioned as one of the EEC's foundational goals in Article One of the Treaty of Rome, although officials in Brussels are often surprised when I point this out, the fact having slipped from their collective awareness. The EU was always protectionist with regard to coal, steel, textiles and, above all, agriculture. This attitude stood in the way of trade relations with many developing states, especially those that depend on agrarian exports. At the same time, Brussels tends to see trade policy as a tool of diplomacy, rather than as a way to enrich the consumer.

For example, many American tech firms have found themselves on the receiving end of hostile Brussels rulings, including Microsoft, Google and Apple. Some put it down to the EU's constant regulatory itch, its determination to leave a mark on everything, but it has just as much to do with deliberate anti-American protectionism. As Günther Oettinger, the commissioner in charge, put it when launching a 'comprehensive investigation' into the role of Internet platforms in 2015, the EU aimed to recover its 'digital independence' from the United States.

In other words, from foodstuffs and commodities to digital technology, the EU's inclination is to protect its vested interests, rather than to promote global commerce.

The clearest way to quantify the EU's protectionism is by measuring, not the total number of trade deals it has, since, as we have seen, these are weighted toward small European states and territories including Andorra, Monaco and San Marino. Let us consider instead, as Martin Durkin did in his magisterial film *Brexit: The Movie*, the total size of the economies with which the EU has trade accords.

Taking the list of treaties registered with the WTO, and totting up the GDP of the countries concerned, we find that the EU has trade deals with economies worth, in total, £5.23 trillion. To put this in context, the equivalent figure for Norway is £19.1 trillion, for Australia £25.6 trillion, for Switzerland £29.2 trillion.

Now let's be more generous, and count the EU as if it were a set of twenty-eight different countries all enjoying free-trade agreements with one another. Even by this measure, counting the EU as trading with itself, so to speak, we still get a value of only £18.1 trillion, compared to £35.5 trillion for Singapore, £45.2 trillion for South Korea and £50.3 trillion for Chile.[31]

Here is Britain's real opportunity. In any trade talks, negotiators divide the economic sectors into 'defensive interests', where they want to restrict foreign competition and 'offensive interests', where they want to prise open the other side's markets. Britain's defensive interests are few; but the EU's are many, and have until now stood in the way of global trade deals. Worse, from a British perspective, EU trade deals are heavily weighted toward goods rather than services – in other words, to the interests of the industrial Continental states rather than the UK.

Britain will soon have the opportunity to sign genuinely liberal accords with like-minded countries. Consider, first, those states which are closest to us in terms of their approach to property rights, free markets

31 WTO – http://rtais.wto.org/UI/PublicMaintainRTAHome.aspx;
World Bank – http://data.worldbank.org/indicator/NY.GDP.MKTP.
CD (GDP figures)

and the rule of law. It should be a priority to sign comprehensive trade deals with states in this category, including the United States, Canada, Australia, New Zealand, Hong Kong, Singapore and Chile.

Since the referendum campaign, it has become clear that the US–EU trade talks, known as the Transatlantic Trade and Investment Partnership (TTIP), are highly unlikely to result in any deal. Germany's economics minister, Sigmar Gabriel, said out loud in August 2016 what everyone connected to the process had long since privately accepted: 'Talks with the United States have failed.' Fourteen rounds of negotiations have produced no agreement. France, in particular, remains resolutely opposed to opening up either its food or its audio-visual sector. Understandably, this has prompted many in the United States to call for the prioritization of a bilateral deal with Britain, where the obstacles in the way of ratification are minor. It would, in Paul Ryan's phrase, 'be easier to do'.

Something similar is true, more surprisingly, of Canada. I say 'more surprisingly' because the Canada–EU deal was concluded some time ago. However, because it was defined as an area of 'mixed competence', it had to be ratified by the twenty-eight member states, rather than simply approved by the European Commission. Two member states, Romania and Bulgaria, announced that they would not ratify the accord unless Canada restored visa-free access to their nationals.

Rather to their surprise, Canada refused to back down. It had imposed visas for a reason. Large numbers of Romanians and Bulgarians, generally of Roma origin, were travelling visa-free to Canada and then making bogus asylum claims, at huge cost to the Canadian taxpayer. Since more than half of Canada's total trade with the EU is, in fact, with the United Kingdom, Canada has indicated that it will happily sign a trade agreement with the UK and wait to see whether the rest of the EU will follow.

It's a similar story around the world. Before the referendum, many governments, evidently in response to a direct plea for help from David Cameron, urged Britain to stay in the EU. Now those same governments are cheerfully indicating their keenness to sign bilateral trade deals with the UK.

By opening our markets to agriculture and textiles, in particular, we won't just give our citizens a boost in disposable income, and thus stimulate our economy. We will also facilitate trade with many Commonwealth and developing nations. India, for example, is a vast market, with a huge textiles industry. It has also been pushing for easier visa access for those of its nationals wanting to work in Britain, particularly as computer programmers.

Britain is the third-largest investor in India, and many of the UK companies that have invested heavily there, such as JCB, backed the Leave campaign. India, conversely, is the third-largest investor here, owning more in the UK than in the other twenty-seven EU states combined. These investment flows reflect our natural commercial interests: there are 1.4 million Britons of Indian origin, and India is a common-law and (for business purposes) English-speaking country. When it comes to trade, though, a very different regime prevails, because Brussels is in charge rather than London. Tata must pay tariffs on what it exports from the UK to India; JCB on what it exports from India to the UK.

In fairness, not all the protectionism has been on the EU side. For much of the post-independence period, India pursued policies of import substitution and self-sufficiency ('swadeshi'). Since the 1990s, though, India has been opening its markets and enjoying commensurate growth. It has free-trade agreements in place with countries all over Asia and the Americas, but its trade talks with the EU have been going on without outcome since 2006.

Obviously, each country has its own conditions

and its own interests. But Britain's general inclination should be toward the lowering of trade barriers, bilaterally or multilaterally when possible, unilaterally when necessary. In practice, no large country has ever succeeded in eliminating all its trade barriers, though Britain came pretty close in the nineteenth century, and benefited immensely. Still, we should at least make free trade and open competition our objective in principle, something to aim at even if we will necessarily sometimes fall short.

One intriguing suggestion that arose at a G20 finance ministers' meeting shortly after the referendum is that Britain might apply to join the Trans-Pacific Partnership (TPP), a trade deal that brings together several states around the Pacific Rim. While Britain is obviously not a Pacific nation, it enjoys unusually close relations with several of the potential signatories, including the US and Canada, Australia and New Zealand, Malaysia and Singapore.

In fact, the TPP is at least as much about harmonized regulation as about free trade. Indeed, tellingly, it doesn't even have 'free' or 'trade' in its title. Although it has positive elements, it also shows signs of having been unduly influenced by cartels. Still, the fact that several TPP members were enthusiastic about British participation is an encouraging sign.

Britain might do better to explore joining NAFTA, an idea that has been mooted in the US and in Canada since the 1990s, but that has always run up against the concrete wall of our EU obligations. NAFTA is, in some ways, the last classical free-trade area, the last agreement built on the principles of mutual recognition and open competition.

British membership of NAFTA was repeatedly proposed in the US Senate by a band of free-traders including Orrin Hatch, Phil Gramm and Gordon Smith. It would, in the current climate, be especially popular in Mexico and Canada, where there are fears that Washington's attitude to free trade may change under the next administration.

NAFTA membership wouldn't simply be good for Britain and for the existing states. It would also hugely boost moves toward global free trade. Norway and Iceland have often mulled some form of association with NAFTA, and there has been semi-official talk of an EFTA–NAFTA tie-up. If other geographically European states were to join alongside Britain, the failure of TTIP might be compensated by the emergence of something better: a transatlantic free-trade area based on the free circulation of goods and services rather than on corporatism and the raising of barriers to entry.

Britain's withdrawal from the EU opens the possibility of a vast and benign change in global trade. The slide away from liberalization and toward standardization might be reversed, and trade talks given a massive boost. The simple fact of a G7 economy opening its markets, including in commodities, textiles and food, would make possible a series of deals that are currently not feasible.

Incidentally, it would be in the interests of the EU twenty-seven to have a free-trading Britain on their doorstep. Not all the Continental governments share our enthusiasm for open competition, though some very much do. In reality, the EU will retain some official and some unofficial barriers, ranging from the Common Agricultural Policy to Commissioner Oettinger's digital protectionism. But even protected markets benefit from having open and competitive trading partners.

As its trade talks – or, strictly speaking, its informal discussions – with the rest of the world get under way, Britain should begin similar talks with its EU allies, first unofficially and then, from March, through Article 50.

Our goal, as already indicated, should be the Owen/Bruegel model of a two-tier Europe: a political core based on the euro, and a wider market around it. If that turns out to lack support, then we should simply offer to maintain free trade, on the basis that we will keep in force – or replicate, if necessary – those EU rules that prevent discrimination against goods or services on grounds of nationality. Very few people object to this aspect of the EU's single market, which prevents vested interests from conspiring against consumers.

Remember that the two-year limit is an incentive for both sides to reach a deal. On the day that Britain leaves the EU, we will become its largest export market. A failure to reach a deal within the two-year timetable, which would risk the re-imposition of tariffs, would be far more detrimental to the EU than to British exporters, for the simple reason that we run a large and permanent trade deficit with the EU, only partly offset by our surplus with the rest of the world.

There is, in short, every reason for both sides to seek a mutually beneficial arrangement in good faith. The idea that Britain might lead an outer group of countries, standing outside political union, but linked to the EU through the nexus of free trade, offers the EU twenty-seven potential gains. It solves the 'Turkish problem': how to deal with a strategically and economically important partner whose political direction precludes EU membership. It allows for the creation of a more prosperous and better-regulated European market than the current haphazard set of overlapping deals. It means that the federalists can pursue their goal with Britain and other neighbouring countries standing by as political supporters and military allies, rather than as grudging foot-draggers. It is, in short, a prize worth aiming for, a consummation devoutly to be wished.

The question of our external relations, however, cannot be divorced from that of our domestic policies. If, for example, we offer to recognize other countries' standards, there are implications for our own regulatory regime: we would have to ensure that our own producers were not handicapped vis-à-vis their competitors. If we choose to cut tariffs, we need to ensure that Britain is a place where foreigners want to do business. If we opt out of Brussels corporatism, we must ensure that we do not replicate it in Whitehall.

Having taken back control, how can we use it to maximum effect? What new opportunities will open up? Remember that leaving the EU was not an end in itself, but a means to an end, that end being a freer, more democratic and more prosperous Britain. What might such a Britain look like?

6

GLOBAL BRITAIN

L ET ME CONJURE a vision for you – a vision of the United Kingdom in the year 2025. We have become Europe's foremost knowledge-based economy; we lead the world in biotech, law, education, the audio-visual sector, financial services and software; new industries – from 3D printing to driverless cars – have sprung up around the country; older industries, too, have revived as energy prices have fallen back to global levels – steel, cement, paper, plastics and ceramics producers have become competitive again.

We stand at the centre of a global trading nexus, having opened our markets to the chief exports of developing nations. We are members of EFTA and NAFTA – indeed, our dual membership has catalysed a progressive fusion of those two great classical free-trade areas – and we simultaneously enjoy comprehensive free trade with the EU, though we no longer have a say in setting its standards.

In many areas, whether because of economies of scale or because rules are largely set at a global level, the UK and the EU continue to adopt the same technical standards. But we are now free to disapply those regulations where the cost of compliance outweighs the benefits.

The EU's Clinical Trials Directive, for example, had wiped out a great deal of medical investigation in Britain. Outside it, we again lead the world in clinical research. Opting out of the EU's e-commerce restrictions has turned Hoxton into the software capital of the world. Britain is no longer hampered by Brussels restrictions on sales, promotions and e-commerce.

Other EU regulations, often little known, had caused enormous damage. The REACH Directive, limiting the import of chemical products, had imposed huge costs on manufacturers. The bans on vitamin supplements and herbal remedies had closed down many health shops. London's art market had been brutalized by EU rules on VAT and retrospective taxation. All these sectors have revived.

Financial services are booming – not only in London, but in Birmingham, Leeds and Edinburgh, too. Eurocrats had never much liked the City, which they regarded as parasitical. Before Brexit, they targeted London with regulations that were not simply harmful but, in some cases, downright malicious: the Alternative Investment Fund Managers Directive, the ban on short selling, the Financial Transactions Tax, the restrictions on insurance. After Britain left, the EU's regulations became even more heavy-handed, driving more exiles from Paris, Frankfurt and Milan to London. No other European city could hope to compete: their high rates of personal and corporate taxation, restrictive employment practices and lack of support services left London unchallenged.

Other British cities, too, have boomed, not least Liverpool and Glasgow, which had found themselves on the wrong side of the country when the EEC's Common External Tariff was phased in in the 1970s. In 2016, the viability of our commercial ports had been threatened by the EU's Ports Services Directive, one of many proposed rules that was being held back so as not to boost the Leave vote. Aimed at the large, state-funded ports on the Continent, such as Rotterdam, Hamburg and Antwerp, that law would have done huge damage to Britain's smaller and private commercial ports. With that threat lifted, the UK has again become a centre for world shipping.

After we left the Common Agricultural Policy, we were able to subsidize our own farmers rather than their continental competitors. Instead of paying £4.6 billion a year into the CAP and getting £2.9 billion back, we could afford to support our producers more generously. British farmers, always more open to technology than their EU rivals, now export all over the world. Meanwhile, pulling out of the Common Fisheries Policy meant we could restore control of our territorial waters, out to 200 miles or the median line. For the first time in thirty years, our fish stocks are a great renewable resource.

Shale oil and gas came on tap, almost providentially, just as the North Sea reserves were depleting, with most of the infrastructure already in place. Outside the EU, we have been able to augment this bonanza by buying cheap Chinese solar panels. In consequence, our fuel bills have tumbled, boosting productivity, increasing household incomes and stimulating the entire economy.

Our universities are flourishing, taking the world's brightest students and, where appropriate, charging accordingly. Their revenues, in consequence, are rising, while they continue to collaborate with research centres in Europe and around the world.

The number of student visas granted each year is decided by MPs who, now that they no longer need to worry about unlimited EU migration, can afford to take a long-term view. Parliament also sets the number of work permits, the number of refugee places and the terms of family reunification. A permit-based immigration system invites the world's top talent; and the consequent sense of having had to win a place competitively means that new settlers arrive with commensurate pride and patriotism.

Unsurprisingly, some other European countries have opted to copy Britain's deal with the EU, based as it is upon a common market, rather than a common government. Some of these countries were drawn from EFTA (Norway, Switzerland and Iceland all joined us in the new arrangement with the EU, known as the Continental Partnership). Some came from further afield (Serbia, Turkey, Ukraine). Some followed us out of the EU (Ireland, Denmark, the Netherlands).

The United Kingdom now leads a twenty-two-state bloc that forms a free-trade area with the EU, but remains outside its political structures. For their part, the EU twenty-four have continued to push ahead with economic, military and political amalgamation. They now have a common police force and army, a pan-European income tax and a harmonized system of social security. The remaining twenty-four nations are – to all intents and purposes – ceasing to exist as independent states, instead becoming units within a federal Europe.

Some in the EU resent the arrangement. They protest that Britain has become Hong Kong to their China, Singapore to their Malaysia: a competitive, deregulated, off-shore economy that attracts investment through lower taxes and less burdensome rules. Others recognize that Britain's openness to global trade benefits the entire region. A prosperous neighbour is a better customer, and the UK remains by far the EU's single largest export destination. In any case, a measure of competition is in everyone's interest.

As the great Scottish Enlightenment philosopher David Hume put it as long ago as 1777:

> Nothing is more usual, among states which have made some advances in commerce, than to look on the progress of their neighbours with a suspicious eye, to consider all trading states as their rivals, and to suppose that it is impossible for any of them to flourish, but at their expence. In opposition to this narrow and malignant opinion, I will venture to assert, that the encrease of riches and commerce in any one nation, instead of hurting, commonly promotes the riches and commerce

of all its neighbours; and that a state can scarcely carry
its trade and industry very far, where all the surrounding
states are buried in ignorance, sloth, and barbarism.

It works both ways: Britain has a stake in the
success and prosperity of its EU neighbours even after
departure; and most Continental politicians recognize
that the reverse is also true.

In geopolitical terms, the apt parallel is not with
Hong Kong or Singapore, but with Canada. Like
Canada, Britain has a federal state on its doorstep
with around ten times its population. Like Canada,
it enjoys the tightest relationship with that federation
commensurate with full sovereignty. Britain remains
a close military, political and economic ally of the EU,
not only through its membership of the wider, non-
political European market, but also as a committed
participant in NATO and the Council of Europe. But,
like Canada, it is independent, and not subject to the
federal jurisdiction which overrides state jurisdictions
in its neighbour. Just as the United States and Canada
have settled naturally into a working relationship so
close that it is rarely questioned, so the EU and Britain
take co-operation for granted.

So much for the ideal. How do we get from here
to there? What policies do we need to pursue, both in

terms of international trade and domestic economic reforms, to realize it?

The issues of trade and domestic reform are linked. Britain can now open its markets in a way that EU membership has hitherto precluded. But, in order to succeed as a global economy, it will need to make itself attractive as a place to do business. The most open economies in the world, such as Singapore and Hong Kong, know that they must also be lithe and attractive in terms of their regulatory regimes, tax rates, welfare systems and employment laws.

Let's start with trade. We have already touched on the superiority of mutual product recognition over standardization. It is far better to say, 'If this item has been approved for sale in Australia (or wherever), then that's good enough for us' than to make a common standard the precondition for commerce. Why is it better? Because it allows for more pluralism, more competition and more consumer choice. Or, to put it the other way around, it prevents cartels of producers using the regulatory system to build barriers to entry and establish monopolies.

But what if there is a problem with the product? There are two reasons that regulations are generally imposed: either to ensure consumer safety; or to reduce some externality, such as exploitative child labour or harm to the environment. Let us deal with them in turn.

There should be a presumption of innocence when it comes to selling goods or services. A pharmaceutical company doesn't want its customers to be poisoned; a car-maker doesn't want its customers to be maimed; a bank doesn't want its customers to be broke. Even the angriest anti-capitalist protesters, determined to see only black motives in the private sector, must concede that injuring your clients is bad for business.

In any case, there are strong and effective mechanisms in our common law for the redress of grievances. If a company or an individual misleads you about the product you are buying, you have recourse under the laws of tort. In many cases, there will also be an element of self-regulation by the industry, aimed at guaranteeing standards that go beyond the prevention of false descriptions.

The question is whether there needs to be government regulation on top of the basic legal protections enjoyed by all citizens. What if, for example, the product or service in question is a complex one – one that no individual consumer could fairly be expected to understand before buying? What about, say, banking? Should the government require banks to hold a certain level of assets by law? Should it force them to advertise their services according to a particular format?

Well, here's the thing. Contrary to popular belief, the last financial crash happened at a time when banks had never been more regulated. The guidebook on how to comply with the regulations – let alone the regulations themselves – was 1,050 pages long. With the possible exception of nuclear energy, no sector was more subject to government rules than financial services. That those dense pages did not prevent the crisis is a matter, sadly, of observable fact. The question is whether they actually made the crash more likely, by replacing a culture of conscience with one of compliance.

A hundred years ago, when banks were only lightly regulated, the onus was on the customer to make a judgement. People understood that there was a trade-off between return on their capital and a small risk of default. Generally, the higher the rate of return, the greater the risk. Banks often used to advertise the amount of capital they kept in reserve as a way of attracting customers.

Today, by contrast, investing is a highly regulated business. Buying into any kind of savings fund generally involves being sent a very long document which you won't read, but which creates the impression that someone somewhere has done the risk assessment for you. And, in the sense of ticking boxes, they have; but that doesn't mean that your investment is actually safe. The reaction of almost every government body that lost its savings with the collapse of Icesave was the same: 'But we followed Treasury guidelines!' As a rule, the more any organization is obliged to follow the dots and commas of a lengthy rulebook, the less space there is for individual discretion, judgement or common sense.

I gave the example of financial services because it is so often cited by supporters of regulation, but the principle is a general one. If people are encouraged to believe that someone else is on top of the risk, they are less likely to engage their own critical faculties. Meanwhile, the bureaucracy supposedly in charge of the risk assessment almost inevitably becomes more concerned with justifying its budget than with carrying out its notional function.

Regulation, in short, can make things riskier. One experiment carried out in the Canadian Rockies suggests that removing all warning signs from mountain roads actually reduces the number of accidents. The signs subliminally tell drivers that someone else is looking after the risk, so when they reach a stretch with no warnings, they unconsciously relax. With no signs at all, people are on their mettle, and drive more carefully throughout. Some Dutch municipalities have gone further, not only removing signs but even removing pavements and mixing pedestrians and vehicles. Result? Fewer accidents.

As for driving, so for shopping. Government ordinances are a remarkably ineffective way to promote consumer safety – even when that is their genuine intention. More often, in practice, the regulations promoted in the name of consumer safety are, in fact, designed to give a commercial advantage to a given firm or cartel.

This is especially true of regulations decreed from Brussels, where the relative distance between officials and voters opens a space for lobbies and special interests. Consider, to pluck a more or less random example, the progressive restriction, from 2005, of a number of higher-dose vitamin and mineral supplements and herbal remedies. The prohibitions and extra tests were justified by Eurocrats in the name of 'the precautionary principle', but a moment's thought reveals the flaw in that argument. Independent herbalists were, in effect, being asked to prove a negative: they had to show that their products *weren't* deleterious to health. The idea that no herbalist would want to sell a toxic product was dismissed. In reality, the restrictions had been quite openly lobbied for by the large pharmaceutical corporations, which saw an opportunity to enlarge their market share at the expense of their smaller rivals. The big companies could easily afford the compliance costs; the smaller ones were driven out of the market.

Outside the EU, Britain's policy should be that regulations will be brought in only in response to a clearly identified existing problem, and then only proportionately and subject to a sunset clause – in other words, regulations will lapse automatically unless explicitly readopted. That policy should apply equally to imported and domestic goods and services. If someone objects to the import of a product that is on sale somewhere else, it should be up to that person or group to make a convincing case for legislation. I say 'legislation' deliberately. At present, many bans are decreed by semi-anonymous standing regulatory agencies. Arguably, the chief advantage of leaving the EU is that we shall once again be governed by elected representatives, not appointed functionaries.

OK, you may say, it's fair enough to assume that companies don't want to harm their customers, and thereby opening themselves to massive litigation. But what about corporations that harm someone else, or that harm us all indirectly through, for example, environmental pollution?

Here, there is a stronger case for regulation. But

it should be entered into, as the Prayer Book says of marriage, reverently, discreetly, advisedly, soberly. Most lobbyists have learned that the best way to disadvantage a rival is by claiming that something or other is harmful to the environment. Think, for example, of the recent EU ban on high-power domestic electrical appliances, such as vacuum cleaners and hairdryers. The contribution of household appliances to global warming is negligible, as even supporters of the directive eventually admitted. They couched their argument in terms of 'discouraging irrational consumer behaviour', but the real motive was simpler: a handful of manufacturers which happened to meet a particular standard (including Bosch and Siemens) saw an opportunity to extend that standard to competitors which didn't (including Dyson).

That decision may have contributed to James Dyson's decision to vote Leave. Whether or not it did, it would be bizarre if a post-EU Britain retained an arbitrary ban on many of his products. By all means, let the EU regulate its markets; by all means, let it demand that Dyson sells only a low-power version of his inventions there. But don't let it dictate what he can sell to the Brazilians or the Bahrainis – let alone to the British.

The wrapping up of hard commercial interest in eco-friendly language can have literally fatal consequences.

In September 2015, the automobile industry was hit by the worst scandal in its history. It emerged that the German car-maker Volkswagen had been programming its vehicles to cheat emissions tests. Some of Volkswagen's diesel engines were fitted with a software-controlled device that detected the conditions of a laboratory test, and caused the emissions of nitrogen oxide (NO_2) to drop to as little as one fortieth of what would be emitted on the open road.

The discovery was, of course, a terrible blow to the company. But it raised another question: why had the EU, almost uniquely in the world, adopted standards that promoted diesel engines? While the American and Japanese governments were encouraging hybrid and electric cars, the EU struck out in a very different direction, enforcing emissions standards that focused on carbon dioxide (CO_2) instead of nitrogen oxide.

The automotive diesel market was almost dead in the late 1980s, when Volkswagen revived the technology with its turbocharged direct injection engines. European car manufacturers saw a market opportunity, and set about lobbying for Brussels rules that would give them an advantage over their rivals. It wasn't an easy case to make. Diesel emits four times more NO_2 than petrol, and twenty-two times more particulates – the tiny pollutants that penetrate our lungs, brains and hearts. Most consumers still thought of diesel, with reason, as the dirtier alternative. How were car producers like BMW, Volkswagen and Daimler to ask for a protected market share?

Well, they were sly enough not to put the argument in terms of their commercial self-interest. Instead, they focused on the need to reduce CO_2 emissions, and so slow climate change. Although diesel is the filthier fuel in most other respects, it does produce 15 per cent less CO_2 than petrol. And so a massive operation was begun to sell the new standard as part of the Kyoto process. Health risks were overlooked, and the conversation was skilfully turned to global warming.

It worked. During the mid-1990s, the car companies negotiated a deal with the European Commission which prioritized a cut in CO_2 emissions over the more immediate health problems caused by exhaust fumes – an arrangement announced in 1998 by Neil Kinnock, then the transport commissioner.

According to Simon Birkett of Clean Air in London, 'It was practically an order to switch to diesel. The European car fleet was transformed from being almost entirely petrol to predominantly diesel. Britain, along with Germany, France and Italy, offered subsidies and sweeteners to persuade car makers and the public to buy diesel.'[32]

Although few remarked on it, that deal heralded a massive divergence between the EU's car market and the rest of the world's. 'It's fascinating that this essentially transformed the market in Europe and nobody paid attention to it,' says Eugenio J. Miravete, a professor of political economy at the University of Texas and co-author, with María J. Moral of UNED in Madrid and Jeff Thurk of the University of Notre Dame, of a study on the rise of the diesel car in Europe.[33]

The car companies' strategy was successful. Diesel went from less than 10 per cent of the UK market in 1995 to more than half in 2012, with equivalent rises in other EU states. Because the industry had been savvy enough to make its case in terms of climate change rather than commercial advantage, the ministers and pressure groups who might have been expected to scrutinize what was happening tended to give car-makers the benefit of the doubt – right up until the shock of the 2015 Volkswagen revelations.

Let's summarize what happened. The EU, lobbied by a vested interest, adopted rules that killed large numbers of European citizens. Yes, killed. We can't

32 *The Guardian*, 22 September 2015
33 'Innovation, emissions policy, and competitive advantage in the diffusion of European diesel automobiles', 30 September 2015

quantify the fatalities precisely because the cause of death in each case was recorded as cancer or heart failure rather than NO_2 inhalation or particulates emissions. But we are talking about thousands of needless deaths: air pollution kills more people globally than malaria and HIV combined.

No one willed these deaths, of course. The ministers and policymakers believed they were saving more lives by tackling carbon emissions. At worst, they made a utilitarian trade-off. As a senior Department of Transport official later put it: 'To be totally reductionist, you are talking about killing people today rather than saving lives tomorrow.'[34] You could argue that politics is all about making unpleasant decisions, and neither that official nor anyone else knew that Volkswagen had found a way to get around the tests for which it had lobbied.

Nor, of course, were the car companies deliberately setting out to murder people. Their employees are no less subject to self-serving biases than Eurocrats or, indeed, anyone else. It is only human to convince yourself of the morality of something that you happen to find convenient. No doubt the Brussels-based lobbyists acting for the car giants genuinely convinced themselves that they were saving the planet.

34 *The Guardian*, 22 September 2015

Still, facts are facts. EU policy ended up killing many innocent people in the commercial interest of one industrial sector.

Outside the EU, Britain will have an opportunity to get away from the cronyism and corporatism that characterize Brussels decision-making. The surest way to do it is to stop passing so many regulations. And the surest way to do *that* is to remove the power of standing agencies to make law.

Most of us have, at one time or another, infracted some official rule. What is striking is how rarely this rule was a recognizable law, passed by legislators whom we could elect or turf out. If you are, for example, fined by Transport for London for failing to bleep your Oyster card correctly on a bus, you are infringing rules made up by a quango. The level of that fine was not set by Parliament or by the London Assembly. That is how most regulations now work. As the Nobel prizewinning economist F. A. Hayek put it: 'The delegation of particular technical tasks to separate bodies, while a regular feature, is yet the first step by which a democracy progressively relinquished its powers.'[35]

Hayek's observation is, of course, a powerful argument against the EU. But there is no purpose in

35 *The Road to Serfdom*, 1944

bringing power back from the unelected European Commission only to leave it with the unelected alphabet soup of acronyms that make up British quangocracy, from the Food Standards Agency to the Financial Conduct Authority. An open economy requires deregulation; not a haphazard and fitful attempt to scrap burdensome rules, but a structural change to prevent them being generated. And that means restoring power to Parliament.

We'll look at how to strengthen Parliament later on. But let me make one happy observation. The mere fact of ceasing to generate new regulations will, over time, lead to a free and open economy, even if few extant regulations are explicitly withdrawn.

In 2008, along with Douglas Carswell, I wrote a book called *The Plan*, which proposed, among other things, a Great Repeal Bill, which would have a mechanism for crowd-sourcing the measures to be scrapped. I am more sanguine now than I was then about the cumulative effect of ceasing to pass new laws.

Who cares, after all, about the regulations on steamboats or fax machines? They have become redundant as technology has advanced. The state is always playing catch-up with the private sector, seeking to bring each new invention into its orbit.

Consider, for example, electronic cigarettes, a

multi-billion-pound industry that didn't exist a decade ago. It grew up without any regulations beyond the general rules that apply to all commerce: laws on accurate advertising and so on. That fact troubled many tobacco companies. It also troubled regulators around the world, especially in Brussels. Eurocrats couldn't accept that a sector with such a vast turnover should not be covered by EU law. At first they tried to bring vaping under the Tobacco Directive, but that proved impossible, since the whole point of e-cigarettes is that they contain no tobacco. Then they tried to classify the new invention as a health product but, again, it wouldn't work: although it has prevented millions of deaths by encouraging people to switch from cigarettes, no one claims that vaping makes you healthier. Eventually, determined not to let any area escape their jurisdiction, they created a new set of sector-specific rules.

Now entertain conjecture of a time when this no longer happened. Dream of a government which did not regulate new sectors, however much the lobbies and interest groups demanded it. Imagine that an ancient and adaptable common law system was trusted to arbitrate disputes without political intrusion. Suppose that regulations were brought in only proportionately, in response to an identified problem, and solely through the mechanism of open parliamentary votes, rather than through technical standing bureaucracies. Suppose, further, that any such regulations had sunset clauses, meaning that they would lapse after a year or two unless expressly reconfirmed.

Regulations in that country, even if there were no specific repeal programme, would soon become obsolete. Think of one of those ruined Mayan temples in the jungles of Central America, its flagstones smashed by roots, its columns choked with creepers. As the rainforest surges with power, so does the unlimited force of human ingenuity expressed through a free market. There would be no need to dismantle the old regulations; all that would be necessary is to allow the private sector to outgrow them until, like those old Meso-American ziggurats, they were swallowed up in a spray of viridian growth.

Such a country, I think we may fairly assume, would flourish. Its regulatory system would be based around the interests of consumers, not producers. Firms from all over the world would want to trade there. That is the future to which we should aspire. And that is why, when we leave the EU, we cannot remain subject to the jurisdiction of the ECJ as full members of the single market.

On 2 October, Theresa May, borrowing the language of *The Plan*, proposed a Great Repeal Bill to scrap the 1972 European Communities Act, but to transpose its contents into domestic legislation. This makes sense: we will have quite enough to do over the next years without having to sift through forty-three years' worth of EU regulations to see which ones we wish to keep. The prime minister is, so to speak, screwing the tap tightly shut before turning her attention to draining the tub.

There is a case for applying a sunset clause here, too: to build into the Great Repeal Bill a clause providing for all the legislation to lapse by, say, 2025 unless explicitly readopted. Although the regulation will in time become irrelevant, we should seek to speed the process of repeal, and a timetable would concentrate minds in Whitehall.

What applies to regulation applies also to trade barriers. Our ideal should be a tariff-free, unsubsidized, open economy. In practice, such a thing has never existed; but that shouldn't stop us getting as close to it as is practicable.

In some cases, a mutual reduction in barriers will be straightforward, because both sides have a predilection toward free trade. Australia, Canada, Hong Kong, New Zealand and Singapore are the countries which have historically been keenest on untrammelled commerce, but Chile is not far behind, together with the other market-oriented states that, alongside it, form the Pacific Alliance: Mexico, Colombia and Peru.

In other cases, the talks will be more complicated, as there will be protected industries and vested interests. This will inevitably be true of the largest and most populous states, including China and India.

During the recent referendum campaign, I often mentioned that Switzerland, unlike the EU, had a bilateral trade deal with China, and was also independently negotiating one with India. Eventually, the Remain side came back with a retort. Switzerland, it said, had a very lopsided deal with China, a deal which provided for the instant opening of all Swiss markets to Chinese exports, but a reciprocal opening by China in only a handful of sectors. For full equivalent access to Chinese markets across all sectors, Remainers said, Switzerland would have to wait as long as fifteen years.

To which the correct reply is, 'So what?' Or, as we Old Brussels Hands say, 'Et alors?' A partial trade deal with the world's second-largest economy is far, far better than no deal at all. And trade deals do not have to be balanced to be beneficial. While the scrapping of all barriers is the best outcome for everyone, a lopsided deal will still benefit both parties.

Suppose that, rather than phasing in access for

Swiss products over fifteen years, Beijing had insisted on a wholly one-way deal: the right to export without restrictions to Switzerland, but with no reciprocal rights for Swiss exporters. Such a deal would still be advantageous from Switzerland's point of view – less so than a mutual deal, but still advantageous. While cheaper competition from China might be disadvantageous to some Swiss producers, that cost is always – always – outweighed by the advantage to the economy overall.

This is, in many ways, a counterintuitive truth, which is why the case for free trade is not an easy one to make. Most of us can see why buying cheaper goods is advantageous: it frees up more household income to spend on other things, and thereby more time, since we can live at the same standard while working fewer hours. We can therefore see why, when another country's goods become cheaper, that is good news for us as customers.

What we often find difficult is the idea that free trade will boost our national economy even when the country we are trading with can undercut us across the board. Free trade is all well and good, we might say, if it allows us to sell the Chinese our cars while buying their toys. But what happens if they can produce both toys and cars more cheaply than us? What then?

The answer was provided by the economist David Ricardo in 1817, and is known as the theory of comparative advantage. Comparative advantage shows why free trade is always and everywhere beneficial to both parties, however much more efficient one party is than the other. It has been called the only idea in the whole of the social sciences that is both surprising and true and, two centuries on, many people still struggle to get their heads around it.

Here is a simplified version. Suppose that Britain and China produce only cars and toys (Ricardo's original example involved England and Portugal, wine and wool). A British worker takes twelve hours to build a car and twelve to make a consignment of plastic toys. A Chinese worker can make a car in forty-eight hours and an equivalent batch of toys in four.

Common sense tells us that both countries will be better off if Britain concentrates on making cars and China on making toys. If British workers make only cars, they can produce two in a twenty-four-hour period. If Chinese workers concentrate exclusively on toys, they can make six batches. If, on the other hand, each country split its time evenly between the two commodities, then the British worker would produce half a car and half a batch of toys, while his Chinese counterpart makes just a quarter of a car along with three consignments of toys. Total production if the two countries trade is two cars and six sets of toys. Total production if they insist on self-sufficiency is one and a quarter cars and four sets of toys. Trade makes both countries better off.

Now for the surprising bit. Suppose that the Chinese get better at car-making. Suppose their workers, with cheaper materials, lower wages and so on, can now make a car in eight hours, while a British worker still takes twelve. China now enjoys an absolute advantage in the manufacture of both cars and toys. Plainly trade between the two states will be good for China, which is more efficient across the board. But how can it be good for Britain? Won't all our factories close in the face of cheaper competition?

No. Comparative advantage means that China is still better, relatively, at making toys than at making cars. Economic self-interest dictates that China will concentrate on what it does best.

Sure, the Chinese worker can now outperform his British counterpart in the automotive sector. But if China concentrates on toys and carries on importing cars, the total production of one British and one Chinese worker in twenty-four hours will be two cars and six sets of toys. If China insists on diverting time and energy into car-making, net production is (if Britain sticks with cars) three and a half cars and three sets of toys or (if Britain steps up toy-making to make up supply) two and a half cars and four sets of toys. Specialization is still in the interests of both countries. The most economically sensible course for China is to concentrate on toys, where it continues to enjoy a comparative advantage, and to import cars. Its time is more valuable as a toy-maker.

Economists call this the 'opportunity cost'. China pays a high opportunity cost when it builds cars instead of toys. For every car that rolls off its production line, it has given up the chance to make two batches of toys, whereas Britain has given up only one. Every minute spent building cars is a costly diversion of resources for China, but not for Britain.

And now, here's the best part: the more efficient China becomes, the better for both countries. Yes, China will benefit more than Britain does from its productivity gains, but cheaper imports free up more British time to concentrate on what we do best. The thing that most frightens people about free trade, namely cheaper foreign produce, is in reality its chief attraction.

As I say, the idea is counterintuitive, and you generally have to read it through a couple of times to see the reasoning. Think of it, if you like, as China buying cars from Britain rather than from itself because it has better things to do with its time. Or Google 'comparative advantage' and watch one of the several YouTube videos that demonstrate the reasoning more vividly than a few dry paragraphs of text can. I promise you, the logic is ineluctable. Strange as it seems, free trade necessarily benefits all participants.

The fact that comparative advantage is difficult to understand makes it very hard to sell as policy. Our brains, evolved on the savannahs of Pleistocene Africa, are not designed to appreciate a modern market economy. We still have the instincts of hunter-gatherers. We want to provide against famine, to hoard food and possessions. The notion of relying on someone else's exports feels somehow wrong.

In fact, the idea of a country being dependent on imported food – or imported energy, or anything else – is no odder than the idea of a town or village or household having to buy in what it needs. But, somehow, those lines on maps make us feel that there is a natural unit that ought to be self-sufficient. Never mind that the most successful economies on Earth are also the most open, that wealthy city-states like Singapore and Hong Kong are utterly reliant on importing even the most basic necessities, and that their readiness to do so tariff-free has led to a miraculous rise in wealth for their citizens. These facts are up against hundreds of thousands of years of intuition encoded deep in our genome.

And there is a further problem with promulgating free trade – a political one. Open markets generally lead to concentrated losses but dispersed gains. For example, suppose that a free-trade agreement with China led to the import of very cheap steel. Perhaps the steel is cheap because it has been indirectly subsidized by Beijing through artificially low energy costs, free land or other state assistance. British steel cannot compete, and plants in South Wales close.

Overall, the impact on the United Kingdom is still positive. Cheaper steel imports mean that, in effect, the Chinese taxpayer is subsidizing the British consumer. Costs fall in every British factory that uses the new product, leading to cheaper production and greater profit. These factories can take on more staff. Shop prices fall. Household incomes rise. A lot of people are slightly better off.

The trouble is not just that the benefits are spread thinly; it's that the beneficiaries won't attribute their good fortune to the trade policies being pursued by their government. The link is far too indirect and convoluted. The newly unemployed workers in South Wales, by contrast, will know exactly whom to blame, and will vote accordingly. It is this basic asymmetry that drives every tariff, every subsidy, every favour to a vested interest.

The trouble is that when barriers and distortions mount up, the country as a whole gets poorer. The temporary advantage bought by one firm, or one sector, comes at the expense of the economy in general. That is why, over time, open economies always outperform regulated ones.

There is no Platonic ideal of a free-trading state. Some countries get close to it, notably Hong Kong and Singapore. But, even there, there are distortions, hidden barriers, favours to interest groups. None the less, the general trend is clear: the more open the economy, the richer the citizens. Countries with open economies don't insist on reciprocity in trade deals. They don't activate anti-dumping measures or complain when a foreign government assists some industry or other. Hong Kong imports almost all of its food. Its government doesn't care where the food comes from, or whether it is produced at below cost price. If the Thais or the Japanese want to subsidize a Hong Konger's rice, runs the argument, let them.

Although Britain should seek to approximate this approach, I have spent long enough in politics to know that things are never that straightforward. There will always be special pleading from this or that group. 'We are victims of dumping.' 'We just need to be tided over for the next year or two.' 'We're not on a level playing field.' 'We're a strategically vital industry.'

In practical terms, there will end up being some government assistance to sectors that make a good case, or have a disproportionate amount of public sympathy or, indeed, are just good at lobbying. But, if we must have state aid, it should be in the form of direct grants rather than tariffs or trade barriers. It is cheaper, as well as more just and more transparent, for the government to pay a group of producers directly than for it to shuffle off the cost on to consumers by restricting imports.

One obvious example is farming. Outside the Common Agricultural Policy, Britain can offer both consumers and producers a better deal. Removing the EU's tariffs and quotas will cause wholesale food prices to fall back toward world levels. All of us will benefit from lower bills, especially low-income families, for whom groceries are a large share of the weekly budget. That extra household income will stimulate the whole economy. And the removal of tariffs and quotas will make global trade deals easier, thus benefiting all British producers, including farmers.

Still, in a world where every country except New

Zealand (whose conditions are very different) pays some kind of grant to its farmers, it is not realistic to expect British farmers simultaneously to forgo all protection and all direct support. If we are going to open our markets to Canadian wheat and Argentine beef and all the rest, we can hardly leave British producers as the only unsubsidized participants in the market.

There is, after all, a reason that farming is subsidized all over the world. Most countries recognize that land is not just a commodity. Rather, it is part of the common wealth of a nation. To put it more prosily, or more transactionally, Britain, like most countries, has planning laws that prevent landowners from realizing the full value of their assets. We recognize that we have a shared interest in our landscape, so we forbid its proprietors to turn it all into golf courses or housing estates. If the government is effectively forcing property owners to use their land in a particular way for wider benefit, it seems not unreasonable that it should compensate them in return.

That compensation, though, should be as cheap, efficient and easy to administer as possible. It should not take the form of output-based subsidies or trade barriers. By far the most economical form of government support is a straightforward acreage-based payment.

There are, of course, many alternative models of farm support in the world. Some governments tie grants to land use or land quality. Some set out to support particular sectors or to encourage production. Some seek to target help to smaller and poorer farmers. Some offer transferable agricultural bonds.

The argument for a straight grant is not that it is the most ingenious system, or the most progressive or even the fairest. It's that it's the cheapest. Instead of money being lost in administration, inspections and appeals, subsidies are paid uncomplicatedly according to how much land someone owns. No late payments, no measuring of hedgerows, no spot checks, no computer glitches: just basic support.

Here's the good news: outside the CAP, we can afford a more generous grant for farmers while still lowering prices. As a net food importer with relatively efficient and profitable farms, Britain has always been both positively and negatively penalized by the CAP. We pay more into the system than others and get less out of it because our subsidies go disproportionately to producers in France, Poland and elsewhere. Last year, Britain paid £4.6 billion into the CAP and got back £2.9 billion.[36]

36 House of Lords, answer to written question HL3254, 3 November 2015

Those figures indicate that we can make a saving for taxpayers and for consumers while still increasing the basic support for farmers. Taking the money that currently goes to our farmers, but paying it all as an area-based grant and thereby slashing the cost of administering the system, would produce a basic subsidy of between £90 and £100 an acre – more than at present, and in line with, or slightly above, what most other countries pay. For some farmers, this would mean a net decrease when other forms of assistance are taken into consideration; for most, it would mean a moderate increase. But, in any event, it would allow our producers to manage the transition. It would be sensible to guarantee these grants up to, say, 2025, so as to provide a measure of certainty. In politics, no one can make a longer-term promise than that.

There will, inevitably, be other sectors that also succeed in making a case for some state support. Our presumption, though, should be against any such subsidies, whether for energy companies or for banks, and whether in the form of procurement subsidies or of direct grants.

Britain won't, to use the favourite journalistic shorthand, 'become like' Singapore or Hong Kong. Although our legal, institutional and educational systems are in some senses comparable, we are starting from very different places in terms of the structure of our economy, the nature of our welfare system and, most obviously, the size of our population. We can, though, usefully learn from the way in which these territories have unbarred their economies, welcoming traffic and commerce from all over the world. Both states, in consequence, have been transformed from impoverished islands into opulent entrepôts. Neither has any natural resources, yet both have comfortably overtaken Britain in GDP per capita – indeed, Singaporeans are now, on average, twice as wealthy as Britons.

The essence of their success is that they understood that opening your economy is not simply a matter of trade. Your commercial policies have domestic consequences. If you accept goods and products from all over the world, you can't place your own producers under a greater regulatory burden than those overseas. If you want to attract business, you need competitive tax rates, a skilled workforce and a welfare system that helps people into jobs. You need cheap energy to power your economy. You need to prevent housing becoming so expensive that it deters investors. You need an immigration system that incentivizes the most enterprising and energetic people to choose your country over rival destinations.

Leaving the EU is our chance to get those things.

What a terrible pity it would be if, after opening the door and striding out, we end up sitting timidly on the doorstep.

7

AN UNFROZEN MOMENT

I T STILL STANDS as one of the most successful reforms
of all time. During the 1980s, the Chilean state
devolved responsibility for pensions to private providers.
Instead of running a pay-as-you-go system, whereby
state pensions were funded out of general taxation, the
government got out of the picture. Chileans now pay into
one of several competing private pensions funds. They
have the security of owning the pension pot themselves,
rather than depending on a state handout that might
become unviable as longevity increases and the ratio of
workers to retirees falls.

Chileans have benefited hugely from privatization.
Most other governments, if they were commercial
pension providers, would be closed down. A private

company that took as much as they do in taxes, and then paid only the meagre state pensions that citizens get after a lifetime of compulsory contributions, would see its directors sent to prison. Chile, almost uniquely among developed countries, doesn't fleece its workers: competition forces pension companies to provide the best rate they can afford.

Very few Chileans now regret the change. But, although the outcome is celebrated, getting there was far from easy. The problem was the massive one-off cost of the transition. There was a lengthy period during which the government still had to honour its obligations to existing state pensioners without getting the revenue from future pensioners, because they were now paying into the private funds instead.

How did the Chilean state manage that cost? The minister who oversaw the process, José Piñera, went on to lecture all over the world about welfare reforms, and I once had a long conversation with him about how he had handled it.

There was, he explained, no secret formula: the government simply had to economize. In order to make the new pensions system viable, all departments had to trim costs, discontinue programmes, move offices to cheaper parts of Chile. But there was an unlooked-for bonus. Because all ministers had bought into the desirability of the new pensions system, they searched willingly and enthusiastically for cuts. Instead of having to plead with his colleagues for more savings, Piñera found that they were coming to him with ideas. In the end, the savings were actually in excess of what the government needed to bring about the transition. It was, Piñera told me, proof of what can be done when an entire government team feels the urgency of the moment.

Leaving the EU offers us a similar transitional opportunity. In the 1940s, the German-American psychologist Kurt Lewin described how change comes in a three-stage process: the unfreezing of old assumptions, the transformation itself, and then the congealing of different assumptions into a new and comfortable inertia.

Britain is now in what Lewin would have called 'an unfrozen moment'. We have an opportunity to redefine the role of the state, and the relationship between government and citizen, that probably won't come again in our lifetimes.

The changes will be of three kinds. First, there will be reforms that are direct and immediate consequences of leaving the EU. Disapplying the Common External Tariff and adjusting to world prices will transform our economy in a way which, though benign, will present temporary difficulties for some sectors. Second, there will be reforms that are indirect consequences of leaving. Having opted out of EU legal structures, we will have the opportunity to approach regulation in a better way, rejecting corporatism and cronyism. Third, there will be reforms that have no immediate link to Brexit, but which will make our country leaner and lither in a competitive world: changes in our tax and welfare models, for example.

Unfrozen moments have more to do with attitudes than with institutions. Since the vote on 23 June 2016, a touch of steel has crept into our collective soul. Leave and Remain voters are aware that the world is watching to see whether we stumble. There is widespread desire to make a success – a palpable success – of independence.

Our guiding principles as we reshape our government should be localism, thrift and simplicity. Decisions should be taken as closely as possible to the people they affect. Power should be devolved to the lowest practicable level – ideally, the individual citizen but, failing that, parishes rather than counties, town halls rather than Whitehall.

Our starting point should be non-intervention. Unless it can be shown that the state needs to do something – operate underground trains or regulate university admissions or run libraries – it should stand aside. When the state does need to intervene, it should do so in the simplest and cheapest way necessary to meet its goal. When, for example, it needs to raise revenue through taxation, it should seek to optimize the ratio of cash raised to activity disrupted or disincentivized. We shouldn't, in other words, use the tax system to send messages, reward or punish particular groups or advance a social agenda. We should recognize that the complexity of a tax system is as damaging to productivity as the overall tax burden. The tax system – and the welfare system, come to that – should be something that anyone can understand without specialist advice.

The man who created the economic miracle that is modern Hong Kong was a Scottish colonial official called Sir John Cowperthwaite, who served as financial secretary there from 1961 to 1971. His reforms – low taxes, small government, light regulation, free trade – turned one of the poorest places on Earth into one of the richest.

Unlike José Piñera, Sir John did not become a darling of the free-market think- tank scene in retirement, but he was occasionally tempted into giving a lecture, and I once had the chance to ask him what had been the hardest part of his achievement. 'Doing nothing is a full-time job,' he told me. 'Don't imagine that *laissez-faire* means putting your feet up. All officials want to extend their powers, all bureaucracies will grow if they can. To stop it happening, you need to be at your desk before your civil servants come in and still be there when they go home.'

How might we apply Sir John's approach to his native land? Recognizing that governments have great capacity to do harm, but limited capacity to do good, how might we create a freer, more enterprising and wealthier Britain? How, in short, might we move the rocks so that the grass can grow?

Let's start with tax. One of the first ideas floated after the referendum result was that the United Kingdom might substantially lower its rate of corporation tax. At a time when the EU is moving toward a common corporation tax rate, this is an obvious move. Until now, Ireland has been the EU state which has most actively set its tax rates to attract investment. Its corporation tax is 12.5 per cent, which has prompted repeated moves, led by France and Germany, to decree an EU-wide minimum rate. In the meantime, Brussels has found other ways to undo Ireland's advantage. In August 2016, Ireland's low tax deal with Apple was found to be in breach of EU law. The European Commission, on the flimsiest and most tendentious of legal grounds, decided that the firm had to pay accumulated taxes for a series of activities which the Irish government had expressly declared to be exempt.

Outside EU jurisdiction, the UK will be able to do what Ireland is now blocked from doing. It will be in a strong position to attract, not only Apple, but Google, Facebook and the other tech giants previously tempted by the Republic's fiscal regime. (Obviously, Ireland could solve this problem by leaving the EU, but that's beyond the scope of this book.)

Britain should not, however, be in the business of wooing investors through sweetheart deals and exemptions. Rather, we should cut our rate of corporation tax as part of a general package of tax cuts. Potential investors are as interested in low personal tax rates as in low business rates. In Hong Kong, income-tax rates range from 2 per cent for the lowest paid to 17 per cent, averaging at 15 per cent.

Although Britain is not going to reach those rates, it should aim to have lower, flatter and simpler taxes than at present. Both Gordon Brown and George Osborne were fond of complicating the tax system, giving little incentives to this or that pet project, often from no higher purpose than to generate a press release.

The complexity of a tax system is every bit as damaging to competitiveness as the overall tax rate.

The more convoluted the tax code becomes, the more time we have to take off work to comply with it. Tolley's Tax Handbook is now 11,500 pages long, twice what it was when Gordon Brown became chancellor, and the number of tax lawyers has increased commensurately. There isn't a small business in the land that doesn't need an accountant.

The very wealthy, who can afford ingenious tax advisers and high upfront fees, turn this complexity to their advantage, sheltering their assets in various pockets unintentionally created by government schemes. The rest of us then have to pay more to make up what the plutocrats are able to avoid.

One way to think of the tax system is as a massive Swiss cheese. Each hole is an exemption created by a chancellor in pursuit of good headlines – a hole waiting to be filled by the clever accountants who work for Starbucks or Jimmy Carr or any other wealthy company or individual.

If we were to compress the cheese, collapsing all the holes, its overall height would fall substantially. In other words, scrap all the special incentives, rebates and waivers, and you can cut the basic rate. We should, for instance, close the loophole that allows the super-rich to avoid stamp duty by putting their Chelsea mansions in their companies' names. We should end the bizarre exemption from capital-gains tax enjoyed by non-doms. Time spent on legal avoidance would instead be spent productively. Revenues would increase. The rich would pay more, in both absolute and proportionate terms. It works every time.

Between 1980 and 2007, the US cut taxes at all income levels. Result? The top 1 per cent went from paying 19.5 per cent of all taxes to 40 per cent. In Britain, when the top rate of income tax was lowered to 40 per cent between 1988 and 2010, the share of income tax collected from the wealthiest percentile rose from 14 to 27 per cent.

Ah, you say, but that's because the rich are earning more. Well, yes. And, as a result, taxes are lower for the rest of us. You might, of course, agree with Roy Hattersley, who once said that he'd rather have 5 per cent more equality than 10 per cent more prosperity. That is a respectable position, but at least be honest about it. Wealth taxes create more equal, but poorer societies.

Flatter taxes, by contrast, make Starbucks-type dodges both pointless and impractical. I've never really understood why the idea isn't more popular on the Left. Cut everyone's rates and you'll make the rich pay more.

Calling for lower, flatter and simpler taxes, you

might say, is the easy bit. What are the implications for public spending? Even allowing for the fact that lower rates will mean higher revenue over time, how are we to prevent the constant tendency of every department and every quango to spend more?

Rather than listing a whole series of individual savings, let me propose two ways in which the structural pressure for higher taxes and higher spending can be reversed. First, fiscal decisions should be devolved; second, fiscal decisions should be democratized.

The closer decisions are taken to the people they affect, the less waste and duplication results. This is partly a question of having more accountable decision-makers. Countries with small populations tend to have accountable leaders, because they have little option but to be available to their constituents. If an Icelander has strong views about, say, his country's trade deal with China, he doesn't need to sign a petition or fire off an email. He can have a quiet word with the trade minister whose daughter plays netball with his on Thursdays.

I remember, on a visit to Iceland, an MP friend coming to a meeting shocked because, while out canvassing, he had come across a constituent whom he didn't know at all. 'I mean, it wasn't just that we hadn't met – there are a few people in Kópavogur

I haven't met – it's that I didn't know her parents or anything!'

Equally, though, proximate decision-making alters the attitude of voters. Suppose that welfare payments were determined locally – hardly an impossible dream, as they are already administered locally. And suppose that you knew your neighbour was working as an electrician while claiming invalidity benefits. I suspect that your attitude would be very different if you could see the impact in your local tax bill rather than, as nowadays, when he is simply defrauding 'the government'.

In *The Plan*, Douglas Carswell and I proposed scrapping VAT and replacing it with a local sales tax, payable once at the point of retail, at a rate set by the county or metropolitan authority. We had spotted that the amount paid by the Treasury to local authorities happened to be exactly the same as the revenue raised by VAT, and so saw an opportunity to make a clean switch. The idea was that, once we had a local sales tax, there would be competing tax jurisdictions, leading to something Britain has never known before, namely downward pressure on rates.

We chose the mechanism of a sales tax for two reasons. First, because it correlates closely to people's disposable wealth, in the sense that rich people tend to spend more. Every other kind of tax falls unjustly on some group or other: a property tax hits widows and pensioners, a flat charge disproportionately penalizes the working poor, an income tax isn't paid at all by around four in ten people. Which brings us to the second advantage of a sales tax: we almost all pay it, because we almost all buy things, giving us almost all a stake in reducing spending. There would no longer be a situation where a chunk of the electorate had every reason to vote for higher spending, knowing that the bill would be met by other people.

The main obstacle to replacing VAT with a local sales tax is that it was clearly against EU law. Brussels sets permissible indirect rates for its member states and collects a chunk of the revenue. Scrapping VAT was not allowed. Now, though, that is no longer a problem.

Although the local sales tax proposal was not taken up, the broad principle of localism has made considerable advances since *The Plan* was published. Manchester and Birmingham, our largest cities, are acquiring considerable powers of self-government, including over healthcare. It is by no means implausible to consider fiscal devolution to our cities – and, indeed, our counties. New Hampshire has almost exactly the same population as Hampshire: just over 1.3 million people in each case. (I am counting the population of Hampshire County Council; Hampshire as a whole, including the unitary authorities of Portsmouth and Southampton, has 1.8 million people.) The American state is deemed capable of running its own taxes, criminal-justice system, police force and social-security system. Is the English county uniquely incapable of self-government?

Whether fiscal devolution comes in the form of a local sales tax or something else is a secondary issue. The important principle is that there should be a proper link between taxation, representation and expenditure at local level. At present, councils have a perverse incentive to spend more. Three quarters of their money comes from central government, so they have to cut spending by £4 in order to cut council tax by £1. The more prudent they are, the likelier central government is to formulate the grant in a way that penalizes their success. Conversely, the more hopeless they are, and the more deprivation they create, the more their populations become dependent on state handouts, making them even likelier to vote for high-spending parties.

What goes for tax goes also for welfare: we should aim, wherever possible, to localize and simplify. The relief of poverty was a municipal function in

England between the dissolution of the monasteries and the twentieth century. Indeed, it was the chief municipal function: local councils were responsible for administering the Poor Law, and there were several statutes aimed at keeping claimants in their own parishes. The rationale behind these vagrancy laws was two-fold. First, that a man's own neighbours would be best placed to decide whether he was truly needy. If 'vagabonds' could move to neighbouring parishes, ran the reasoning, then 'sturdy beggars' might pass themselves off as invalids and walk off with alms to which others had a better claim. Second, because local ratepayers would be more willing to fund the relief of poverty in their own towns and villages than to pay into a depersonalized system.

As the welfare state has grown larger and more comprehensive, any connection between contributor and recipient has been lost. Partly as a consequence, the modern welfare state has failed to meet its foundational objectives. Grants that were supposed to have a one-off transformative effect have become permanent, as claimants arrange their affairs around qualifying for them. People become trapped by perverse incentives, understandably turning down jobs that, when everything is taken into account, will leave them hardly any better off – even, in a few cases, worse off.

At present, broadly speaking, central government determines eligibility for benefits, and local authorities are responsible for delivering them. Allowing councils to set their own criteria would reduce the unintended consequences. Put bluntly, local decision-making will allow the authorities to distinguish more clearly between deserving and undeserving cases.

The United States carried out a substantial devolution of social services from the federal government to the fifty states in the 1990s – arguably the most successful welfare reform ever carried out by a major industrialized country. The decentralization of decision-making led to more innovation, lower costs, higher rates of employment, a fall in poverty and a general rise in satisfaction from claimants.

Democrats in Congress initially opposed the change on grounds that it would lead to a race to the bottom. And, in a sense, they were right. No state wanted to maintain a generous provision of benefits while others were cutting, lest it become a magnet for every bum and idler in the country. Instead of writing out cheques unconditionally, every state began to experiment with ways to get people into work. Soon, despite his party's misgivings, President Clinton was cheerfully claiming credit for the reforms, which were, in reality, the work of the two Congressional Republican leaders, Dick

Armey and Newt Gingrich. (Sadly, some of their innovations were reversed by Barack Obama as part of the general expansion of the federal government that followed the financial crash, but that's another story.)

Britain may not yet be ready for such a shake-up – although, if Manchester and the other newly empowered authorities make effective use of the competences they are currently gaining, control over welfare might in time follow.

What is already clear, though, is that the once widespread assumption that any reform of welfare was politically impossible – that it was, in the American cliché, the 'third rail' which would deliver a high-voltage shock to any politician who touched it – is no longer valid.

The policies pursued by Iain Duncan Smith during the last parliament were a huge success by the most basic measure – namely, they moved a large number of people off benefits and into work. During the lifetime of the 2010 to 2015 Parliament, the United Kingdom created more jobs than the other twenty-seven EU states put together.

The welfare reforms were not pursued in isolation: abolishing income tax on the first £10,500 (rising to £12,000) that people earned significantly recalibrated the balance of advantage, making part-time work much more attractive. But, in a way that would have seemed unthinkable in the 1980s and 1990s, opinion polls showed consistent support for a Tory government trimming benefits payments.

Sadly, the centrepiece of the IDS reforms has still not happened, namely the idea of wrapping all the various benefits and allowances into a single universal credit. Quite apart from various technical delays, the purity of the original idea was already being lost as various interest groups began to maul the proposal.

A single universal credit would certainly be a further improvement on the current system. Simplification is always desirable. In particular, there is a case for making a single payment available as the state pension, without regard for wealth, circumstances or employment history, a sum that would replace every other payment, from free bus passes to housing benefit. And – a hard thing that needs saying – this sum should, over time, become minimal, just enough to prevent penury, so that people are encouraged to make savings or arrange private or workplace pensions.

New Zealand operates a similar system, paying a low sum to all pensioners, regardless of their means, and thereby encouraging citizens to provide for their retirement without creating the problem of the freeloader, which bedevils every other pensions system. If pensions are tied to what you have paid in, there will always be marginal cases where your thrift is penalized – in other words, where you would have done just as well to make no provision for your old age, to have spent your savings, and to have relied on the state to cover your retirement. These perverse incentives particularly penalize women who have taken stretches away from work as carers. Paying everyone an identical sum, but making it too low to be attractive, is a good way to incentivize private provision.

While Britain was in the EU, there was no way of running such a system without opening it to every other EU national who chose to move to the UK. EU membership effectively ruled out a New Zealand-style 'citizen's pension' and, indeed, called into question the whole notion of a universal credit system, since it was always possible that a future ECJ ruling would entitle half a billion EU nationals to claim it, thereby bankrupting the system. Outside the EU, such reforms are feasible.

The best way to contain the growth in welfare spending, though, is by devolving control, either to local authorities or, through them, to private providers, including churches and charities. That should remain our goal.

The Coalition government's welfare reforms were received approvingly by most voters, despite a massive campaign by their opponents. They were popular for two reasons. First, because the rise in welfare spending under the previous government violated people's sense of natural justice. The idea that no family on benefits should receive more than the average – the *average* – working household struck most people as eminently reasonable. Second, in the aftermath of the financial crash, voters were more responsive that usual to the argument that the country needed to tighten its belt.

Leaving the EU is not akin to the financial crash, obviously. There is, though, a sense that, having made our decision, we should pull together to make it as successful as possible. Once again, people are ready to defer gratification, to make reforms that will lead to greater long-term prosperity.

Still, we shouldn't underestimate the political difficulty inherent in cutting government spending. Ministers face the same problem as they do when eliminating tariffs and trade barriers, only this time it's the costs that are dispersed and the gains that are concentrated. Ending a subsidy, benefit or grant makes a negligible impact on the tax bill of any individual once it has been spread across the entire nation; but it makes a significant impact on the income of the former recipient. That is why it is so much easier to initiate a new grant or government programme than to terminate an existing one.

Once we have lower, simpler, flatter and more local forms of taxing and spending, few will look back. None the less, getting there will involve some tough arguments. We must not allow the unfrozen moment to solidify.

The same is less true of measures to reduce the cost of living: these will encounter some resistance from vested interest groups, but ought to enjoy general popularity from the start.

What are the four main items of household expenditure? For most of us, they are food, fuel, housing and tax. Tax is the one we tend to notice least, because it is taken from us in a series of surreptitious, sundry and convoluted ways: through PAYE, through VAT, at the petrol pump and so on. But the consolidated tax bill of most working households is not only heavier than the other three large items; it is typically as heavy as all of them combined.

So, how to exploit the opportunities of withdrawal? We have already touched on how food prices will fall outside the EU, and looked at how tax, too, might come down. What of energy and housing costs?

One immediate consequence of leaving the EU is that we will be able to decide for ourselves how to exploit the vast pool of shale gas under our soil. Shale energy deposits in Britain are among the largest in the EU which, yet again, gives us national interests that diverge from the mean. The EU has been energetically searching for new ways to restrict shale exploitation, with rules being partly set by states that have negligible reserves.

All economic growth comes down to energy. It drives everything else. First, that energy was largely human – hence the slave empires of the Bronze Age; then it shifted to horses and oxen; then to coal; then to oil. It was Britain's immense good fortune to happen upon large coal deposits just as industrialization was getting under way in the eighteenth century. And what was true then is true now: fracking has led to a sharp fall in US energy prices over the past decade, hugely boosting the economy despite a measure of government mismanagement.

Unlike nuclear energy or renewables, shale requires no government subsidy. On the contrary, it generates large tax revenues. Unlike wind farms, it requires an installation no larger than a garage. Yes, there is a certain disruption involved in building that installation; but Britain is lucky enough to have an extensive network of gas pipelines already in place.

Cheaper energy means that factories make more

things. It means that goods can be shipped at a lower cost. It means that consumers have more disposable income, and so can buy more stuff, or launch new enterprises. A country with artificially high energy bills places itself at a permanent disadvantage in the global race.

Even if we discount shale gas, the EU already places its member states under that handicap. As a result of EU policy, Britain has some of the highest electricity and gas bills in the world. Brussels drives up prices in two ways: through setting renewables targets and, since 2010, through direct legislation. As a result, a medium-sized business in the EU pays 20 per cent more for energy than an equivalent firm in China, 65 per cent more than one in India and 100 per cent more than one in the United States.[37] These artificially high energy prices have already closed most of Britain's steel industry, and now threaten other high-energy manufacturing sectors. And not just our manufacturers: in 2012–13, the NHS spent an extraordinary £630 million on energy bills.[38]

It is of course true that the world is seeking to reduce carbon emissions, and Britain will presumably

37 European Commission Staff Working Document, 'Energy prices and costs report', 17 March 2014
38 TaxPayers' Alliance, *Research Note 133: Energy and Water Bills in the NHS*, 21 November 2013

remain part of that global effort after leaving the EU. But the EU doesn't simply set a target for emissions cuts and leave it to the member states to meet it. That would be to accept the supremacy of the approach agreed at the 2015 Paris Climate Summit which, being global, makes regional blocs largely irrelevant. Instead, Brussels supports specific forms of alternative energy in a way which has the incidental effect of purchasing the loyalty of those who supply it.

Where I live, in beautiful countryside on the Hampshire–Berkshire borders, there is a widespread phenomenon that I can only think to call 'upper-class welfarism'. The talk at dinner parties will often turn to (say) how you can get £30,000 a year from the government by installing a woodchip boiler, which can then conveniently be used to heat your swimming pool. Because most alternative energy schemes benefit people who own woods or suitable sites for wind farms, they end up becoming a form of regressive taxation. People on low and medium incomes pay higher electricity bills to subsidize landowners, many of whom then have an incentive to support the existing racket. Not in every case, of course: plenty of landowners voted Leave, just as some MEPs voted Leave. In general, though, the current system of EU energy subsidies works very well for the very rich.

What it is far less useful for is reducing carbon emissions. As Friends of the Earth points out, the impact of EU policy is, in effect, to force manufacturers and other businesses to outsource to places with far lower environmental standards. British industrialists naturally agree. So, come to that, does the British government. According to a study by the Department of Energy & Climate Change, just two EU rules are responsible for 9 per cent of the energy costs incurred by energy-intensive businesses today – a figure that would have risen to 16 per cent in 2030 had we remained members.[39]

The closure of most of Britain's steel mills in 2015 had more than one cause, but uncompetitive energy prices were the underlying problem. Although campaigners from the industry focused on Britain's inability to activate anti-dumping rules against China, China's advantage was itself a product of the massive differential in power costs. Outside the EU, we could theoretically support our steel plants either through anti-dumping measures or through direct grants. Both would be harmful to the British economy overall though, if we end up giving in to political pressure,

39 The Emissions Trading Scheme and the Renewables Obligation. Department of Energy & Climate Change, 'Estimated impacts of energy and climate change policies on energy prices and bills'.

subsidies are less damaging than trade barriers. But we shouldn't do either.

Immediately after the referendum result, Tata, which had previously declared that it was pulling out of South Wales, announced it was reconsidering that decision in the light of a more competitive exchange rate. If the UK could offer cheaper energy as well as a cheaper pound, our steel industry won't need support. This should be even more true if the current trend toward specializing in more expensive and niche forms of steel continues.

What goes for steel goes for every other energy-intensive industry. Lower production costs will give a massive fillip to several sectors, including cement, ceramics, glass and paper.

Nor will it be just cheaper energy. Disapplying other burdensome EU regulations will give manufacturing in general a competitive boost. For example, the chemical industry has been hugely disadvantaged by a little-known regulation known as REACH. Because REACH is technical and complicated, it rarely featured in the lists of onerous regulations which Eurosceptics wanted to scrap; but it arguably imposes more unnecessary costs on British manufacturers than any other single EU rule, by prohibiting a series of imports – or, rather, by forcing companies to purchase their materials much more expensively.

Scrapping directives like REACH, at the same time as allowing energy costs to drift back to world levels, will strengthen the British manufacturing sector which, contrary to popular belief, has managed a successful transition from mass production to high-end and specialist products, and which is growing in absolute volume while retaining its share of the overall economy.

But what of those manufacturers who depend on EU markets? What of those sectors where the ease of export to the EU's single market outweighs the costs of regulation? I am prepared to accept that there are some companies, possibly even some entire sectors, in this category. The obvious candidates are our automotive and aerospace sectors.

It's true that, in these as in other industries, spokesmen have changed their tune since the referendum. Even Nissan, which is owned by the French firm Renault and which was repeatedly wheeled out by Remain campaigners to warn against Brexit, now says it is 'reasonably optimistic'.[40] None the less, there is an argument that, for a firm that sells as much or more to the rest of the EU than it does to domestic consumers, full participation in the single market, or even in the customs union, might make sense.

40 BBC News, 5 August 2016

To remind ourselves of what these terms mean, the single market is a set of common rules applied to the domestic economies of all participating members. EU states have these rules set for them by Brussels institutions; EEA states such as Norway and Iceland are obliged to apply them, though they do so through their own legislative mechanisms; and Switzerland, which is in EFTA but not in the EEA, has voluntarily agreed to harmonization in some but not all fields.

Britain, I have already argued, should not accept any mechanism for the automatic imposition of single-market regulations, but should aim, rather, at a Swiss-style arrangement where it can opt in issue by issue.

A customs union, as we saw earlier, is a unified trade bloc with a common external tariff and exclusive competence to strike trade deals on behalf of its member nations. Opting out of the common external tariff is one of the chief advantages of leaving the EU: it will mean more trade with non-EU markets and a fall on the cost of living at home.

There is, though, precedent for partial membership of the EU customs union. Some neighbouring states and territories opt into it for particular sectors. Turkey, for example, is a partial member of the EU customs union, contracting out its trade policy in certain areas while retaining its seat at the WTO.

What would it mean if Britain opted for something similar? What if, in other words, we decided that our car and aeronautical industries did so well out of the European market that even the marginal extra form-filling faced by Swiss and Norwegian exporters would damage them? Well, in theory, Britain could do as Turkey has done. It would mean that, if we signed a trade deal with Australia, it wouldn't cover cars. Our cars would continue to face tariffs in Australia (unlike, say, Japanese cars, because there is an Australia–Japan FTA), and would also continue to have their present arrangements with the EU – with the mild difference that British MEPs would no longer have 9 per cent of the votes when the rules were set in Brussels.

My preference is to go for a clean break, a global future. But I am prepared to be persuaded by the industries concerned. If there genuinely is an over-whelming case for keeping the current arrangements – if that is the view of a company's shareholders, not of its Brussels-based lobbyists who, from self-interest, understandably want to remain subject to every EU law – then we should be prepared to build that into our negotiating position.

A trading arrangement need not be all or nothing. It is possible to agree to a common tariff regime for, say, traditional cars, but not for driverless cars.

Indeed, before the renegotiation, I had proposed that Britain could simply outgrow the Common Commercial Policy by exempting new industries from it. If EU tariffs continued to apply to coal, steel and textiles, but not to new technologies, they would eventually cease to matter. The referendum has now reversed that situation. Instead of an assumption that we are inside the customs union except where we negotiate an exemption, there will be an assumption that we are outside unless, for reasons of shared interest, we agree to continue in a particular sector. I look forward to toasting that arrangement with some New World wine which, outside the EU's tariff regime, will be fully 32 per cent cheaper.

There is one more area of government policy that has a direct impact on business and on the attractiveness of the UK as an investment destination, namely housing. British planning laws have given us some of the most expensive property in the world. The distortion affects potential investors both directly, in the sense that a British HQ will be pricier, and indirectly, in that the higher cost of living will oblige them to pay employees more.

Planning laws were introduced for a reason. Britain has a high population density; indeed, England is the most crowded space in Europe. No one wants to see our unique countryside diminished. The trouble is that planning laws are not an effective way to preserve beauty, whether natural or architectural. Much of the development brought in under current planning laws is spectacularly ugly, not least in green-belt land, where the restrictions are most severe. The next time you drive around the M25, look at the scenery on either side of the motorway. Sure, there are some pretty stretches, such as when you pass through the Surrey Hills; but there are also plenty of hideous buildings and warehouses. The M25 cuts through what is supposedly green-belt land; yet less than a sixth of London's green belt is open to the public as green space or has any environmental status.

Government restrictions – in planning, as in every other field of activity – create perverse incentives and encourage operators to make huge profits by lobbying successfully for exemptions. The result is that local populations feel alienated and, more seriously, that bad decisions are made.

Our approach to planning should be the same as our approach to taxation and to welfare: localize and simplify. At present, policy is based on the assumption that local councils won't build any homes unless they are made to. Central government therefore requires local authorities to build a certain number of dwellings, rather as the USSR used to decree the number of bicycles or chocolate bars produced.

What if, instead, there was a presumption in favour of private property rights? What if local councils, rather than having targets, simply had to arbitrate between the interests of the person wanting to build and the impact on his neighbours? What if we could monetize the indirect cost to others in the community of, say, having their view diminished, or of facing more traffic on the road? What if we could allow people to put a price on any disruption caused during construction?

Some US states have hit upon an ingenious way to decide where to site unpopular infrastructure. The undesirable facility – it could be anything from an incinerator to a mobile-phone mast – is offered to eligible counties for a price. Each county is invited to submit a sealed bid saying how much it would want to be paid to host the installation. The county might not like the proposed project at any price, and is not required to submit an offer. The facility is then allocated to the county that has made the lowest bid, and the county authorities are free to use the revenue as they wish, either returning it to local taxpayers or spending it on something else.

That principle could be extended from unpopular

installations to other building projects. The present government is mulling a proposal to make a proportion of the revenue from fracking available to local residents through a council-tax rebate. Why not do the same across the board? Why not allow local communities to put a price on accepting new housing estates? Where there are pristine villages in unspoilt landscapes, very little, if anything, will get built. But in much of the country, building will be far easier. Instead of developers effectively having to invest in lobbying or even indirectly bribing a local authority to redesignate land, and thereby make a guaranteed fortune, larger and more comfortable homes, including whole new towns, will be raised because most people will accept expansion for a price.

The same is true of even the most controversial infrastructure projects, such as airports. Living near an airport unquestionably involves a cost in terms of noise, and every increase in traffic raises that cost. But if the local authority were free to keep most of the revenue raised by the airport, the people living in the area would be able to enjoy well-funded facilities at almost no cost: the airport would more than cover their rates.

In the eighteen years that I have been an elected representative, I have noticed two things about planning decisions. First, they matter more than almost anything else in politics. There is no surer way to fill a village hall than by proposing a new development. Second, they have been largely lifted from the hands of local residents. What bothers people is not simply the fact of having a field turned into more houses, or having HS2 built near by. What truly enrages them is the sense of powerlessness: the sheer frustration of knowing that, even when a development is opposed by their district councillor, their county councillor, their MP and their MEP, it makes no difference.

The Coalition government partially mitigated that sense of frustration by allowing local communities to propose alternative housing plans. When an area is told that it needs to build a certain number of homes, it may now propose to configure them differently and then hold a referendum on which of the two plans to accept. The new mechanism has worked well. Local communities all across my region have risen to the challenge. Local architects, retired planners and public-spirited people with all manner of skills get together. They talk seriously about the number of school places they'll need, about local transport routes, about whether their children will be able to live in the same town or village. Every referendum I have seen in my region has preferred the local plan to the original one.

Local decision-making is, of course, superior to national decision-making. But individual decision-making is better yet. Why not let local landowners or developers make a direct offer to their neighbours? Allow residents to decide, not just where to place new houses, but how many to accept, and for what price.

At a stroke, the frustration that characterizes almost all planning decisions will be wiped away. As with immigration, people will respond more roundedly when they feel they have been listened to, that policy is being made with their consent.

It is one thing to be told: 'A mobile-phone mast will be built on the roof of your local school.' We naturally bridle at being presented with a *fait accompli*. We want to protest and petition. It is quite another thing to say, 'Would you like a small fee in exchange for having the mast – which will, incidentally, mean that your teenage daughter will be able to get reception when she needs you to pick her up at night?' In politics, as in life, people react very differently when you ask politely.

There is one more clear benefit to leaving the EU – one where the ledger is entirely positive – namely, the recovery of our fishing grounds. The British fishing industry has been arguably the single greatest victim of common European policies. Great Britain is surrounded by some of the richest fishing grounds in the world; yet 70 per cent of its fish stocks are outside its control.

An entire way of life has been destroyed. There is not a single major fishing port left between Plymouth and Peterhead, and only 12,000 people now work in the industry. This is not some long-term decay caused by technological change or by overfishing. There has been no comparable decline in the fishing industries of those North Sea states that remained outside the EU: Norway, Iceland, Greenland and the Faroe Islands. The decline is wholly man-made, and stems directly from the surrender of what should have been a major national interest.

Under maritime law, a country's fishing rights extend out to 200 nautical miles or the median line. That is not to say that no vessels may fish in another country's waters. A country may sell a certain size of catch, or the right to fish for a certain period, to trawlers from elsewhere: the Falkland Islands, for example, raise large revenues by selling licences to skippers from East Asia who come for the squid. Likewise, states may come to reciprocal arrangements to preserve numbers. If a certain species spawns in the waters of country A, but reaches maturity in the waters of country B, both countries have an interest in coming to an agreement on total catches – and this is, indeed, what happens when the EU negotiates with neighbours such as Iceland and the Faroes.

The EU's Common Fisheries Policy, however, does not work that way. Negotiated literally hours before the UK application for membership was presented, it defines fish stocks as a 'common resource' to which all member states have 'equal access'.[41] The fish are landed according to a quota system which penalizes the UK especially harshly. By a happy accident of geography, most North Sea fish are in British waters; but the British quota has never come close to reflecting that fact. Why? Because the UN Law of the Sea, extending rights out to 200 miles or the median line, was being negotiated as Britain joined, and came into effect in the North Sea in 1976. Britain's quota was set to reflect previous catches, and was not revised.

The result was that other nations, notably Iceland, were now able legally to exclude British vessels from many of the fishing grounds where they had habitually worked – the cause of the Cod War between Britain and Iceland. But Britain had no equivalent gain in its own waters, because these were part of the EEC's 'common resource'.

Like all common resources, this one was soon plundered. That which no one owns, no one will care

41 Fisheries Regulation 2140/70

for. A skipper will not willingly tie up his boat when he knows that foreign vessels are plying his waters. The Common Fisheries Policy, which is sometimes absurdly defended on grounds of sustainability, has seen a vacuuming up of fish not matched in New Zealand or the Faroes or the Falklands or, indeed, any territory that has clear ownership of its fish stocks, and thus an incentive to treat them as a renewable resource.

Most of the waters being overfished would, but for the EU, have been British. But, under the terms of the CFP, there was nothing we could do. Just as EU membership excludes us from the table when global standards are being set on banking rules or aviation, so the same applies to fisheries.

Let me quote George Eustice who, at the time, was the minister responsible:

The North Sea is economically the most important fishery in the UK. We are Europe's largest producer of mackerel and North Sea cod and haddock are vitally important fisheries. However, fishing opportunities for stocks like mackerel are not even decided by the EU. They are settled at an entirely separate organization called the North East Atlantic Fisheries Commission through the annual Coastal States Meetings. Norway has a seat at the table; Iceland has a seat at the table; the Faroes have a seat at the table. But, extraordinarily, the UK, the country with the greatest interest in the North Sea, is denied a seat at the table because we are a member of the EU. Instead, our technical experts and diplomats are reduced to whispering in the ear of an EU negotiator and hoping they don't mess it up.

On at least two occasions in the past year, EU negotiators have messed it up, unilaterally trading away the interests of Scotland's fishermen in order to give advantages to other EU countries. First, they gave the Faroes increased access to UK waters to catch mackerel and blue whiting. Then, in December, they used UK blue whiting quota as currency to swap for Norwegian Arctic cod which countries such as Germany and Portugal wanted. On the first occasion, the UK was not even consulted and on the second occasion our objections were ignored even though fish in UK waters were providing all the currency for the deals.

Outside the EU, Britain will reassume responsibility for its own waters, and will take its own seat at the table alongside Norway, Iceland and the EU twenty-seven. This is not to say that we shall abolish quotas: they are vital to conservation, and a quota system invented in Iceland to incentivize restraint is now being copied elsewhere. Nor will it mean that we suddenly disregard the rights of other nations that have historically fished in the waters that are now fully restored to our control.

What it will mean is that the balance of advantage tilts heavily back toward the United Kingdom. Instead of having to plead with EU negotiators before international talks, we shall represent ourselves. And, although we shall of course agree quota swaps and similar arrangements with the EU, as with other neighbouring states, we shall be starting with a far larger legal entitlement than now.

We should be prepared to phase the changes in, recognizing the interests of our EU allies. Our aim, though, must eventually be to have control of our own waters so that we can institute an Iceland-style sustainable quota system and start growing our stocks again.

As George Eustice's remarks suggest, Scottish skippers will be among the chief beneficiaries. Restoring sovereignty over agriculture and fisheries directly to the Scottish Parliament – and to the assemblies of Wales and Northern Ireland – would make sense democratically and pragmatically. In these fields, as in most others, decisions are best taken close to the people they affect.

You might be a little bit cynical as we end this

chapter. I have identified tax, food, fuel and housing as the main components of most household budgets. And I have shown why all of them should now fall: tax because of the independence dividend; food because we'll be outside the Common Agricultural Policy; and fuel because we can disapply the EU's most burdensome energy directives. Housing won't become cheaper as a direct consequence of Brexit – which is paradoxical, given that George Osborne claimed house prices would slide by between 10 and 18 per cent before the end of 2018 if we voted Leave. Still, there is every reason to hope that a renewed focus on competitiveness will lead to a long-overdue increase in housing stock – at a time, incidentally, when we are more able to regulate the number of migrants settling in the country.

So why, you might reasonably ask, didn't you hear about these things during the campaign? If leaving the EU really will lead to an appreciable fall in the cost of living, why didn't Vote Leave make more of it?

The answer is that voters have become inured to promises of improvement. It is a sad fact of modern politics that no one believes statistics. Those of us who were running the campaign expected and expect to see a significant rise in disposable income as a consequence of Brexit. We had calculated the likely savings as £933 a year for the average family.[42] Unlike George Osborne's £4,300, our figure was based on a measurable difference between EU and world prices. That extra £933 would have a far healthier stimulant effect on the economy than the repeated bouts of money printing we have seen since the crash.

It would disproportionately benefit low-income families, who spend a higher percentage of their incomes on food and fuel – as well as clothing, which should also become cheaper outside the Common External Tariff. Quite apart from the appeal of social justice, low-income families are likelier to use extra income in ways that stimulate economic growth. But, however we phrased it, our focus groups kept returning the same response: 'Yeah, just another politician's promise.'

A fall in the cost of living will be, if you like, a Brexit bonus, an unlooked-for advantage. The same is not true of what was, according to every survey, the chief motive for Leave voters, namely the restoration of our democracy. Expectations here are high, and we need to ensure that they are met.

42 'Change, or go', Business for Britain, 2016

8

POPULISM VERSUS DEMOCRACY

ONE ADJECTIVE, more than any other, is used in Brussels to describe the Brexit vote. It was, we are told a hundred times a day, 'populist'.

'We have to fight against nationalism,' was how Jean-Claude Juncker responded to the British referendum result. 'We have the duty not to follow populists but to block the avenue of populists.'[43]

Ah, populism. There is no more vicious word in a Eurocrat's vocabulary. He spits it out in the manner of a teenager at a party who has mistakenly taken a swig from a beer can than was being used

43 Speech at the Alpbach Media Academy, 22 August 2016

as an ashtray. Yet he is surprisingly vague about its meaning.

The one thing that he unequivocally understands populism to signify is 'something that other people like, but I don't'. Plainly, in this sense, Britain's vote to leave the EU was populist. But was it really, as so many TV reporters around the world assume, a vote for angry nativism? Was it a British version of the rise of Donald Trump? Or was it, rather, a legitimate reaction to an oligarchic system – a reaction informed by an ancient tradition of representative government?

In Brussels, few are capable of drawing the distinction between democracy and populism. You cannot be a decent Eurosceptic. The only respectable position is to support political integration. Voting against ever-closer union, even if your motivation is an essentially liberal preference for decentralization, open government and anti-corporatism, is *ipso facto* populist.

My neighbour in the European Parliament chamber when I was first elected was a hefty Belgian Christian Democrat. He used the word 'populist' frequently and ferociously, applying it with particular venom to supporters of Flemish independence. I once asked him whether the Flemish separatists weren't simply representing their voters, just as he represented his. 'As politicians we have a duty to lead, not just to do what people want!' he replied. Got it, I said. What you mean by 'populism' is 'having a legislature that broadly reflects public opinion'. In my country, we call that 'democracy'.

Perhaps I shouldn't have been quite so snippy with him. After all, my Belgian colleague had a point that, in a representative democracy, legislators should follow their consciences. A healthy regard for public opinion doesn't oblige us to contract out our convictions. All parliamentarians – trust me on this – go through moments when we think that the majority of our constituents are plumb wrong about something. At these moments, we like to recall Edmund Burke's Address to the Electors of Bristol:

> Your representative owes you, not his industry only, but his judgment; and he betrays, instead of serving you, if he sacrifices it to your opinion.[44]

What we don't like to recall is what happened next. The Electors of Bristol were unimpressed by Burke's characteristically high-minded argument. In particular, they resented the way in which his generous championing of the Irish cause challenged the mercantile interests of their city. The poor fellow was

44 Speech to the Electors of Bristol, 3 November 1774

slung out at the next election. In his private moments, Burke would perhaps have called it populism, though I have no doubt that the Electors of Bristol would have called it democracy.

The essential feature of all populist movements is their belief that an elite is governing in its own interests rather than that of the general population. To make an obvious point, the validity of the populist argument depends on the extent to which that assessment is accurate.

Even in an open democracy, there is a natural tendency for people in power to rig the rules in their own favour, to give themselves an institutional advantage: established political parties passing laws that make it harder for newcomers to challenge them; big corporations using the regulatory regime to erect barriers to entry; public-sector workers ensuring that the system favours producers over consumers; mega-banks persuading politicians to bail them out with taxpayers' money – all these are, in their ways, examples of oligarchy. And all of them are intrinsic to modern politics, because human beings are naturally self-interested. To the extent that they trigger a populist backlash, that backlash might be considered a proportionate and necessary antibody.

To put it another way, a measure of populism is

inherent in any democratic system. The intensity and validity of the phenomenon depend upon circumstances. And that is where the difference lies between mainstream British Euroscepticism and the rise of Podemos and the Front National, the Occupy Movement and the Tea Party, Bernie Sanders and Donald Trump.

British *souverainisme* is not nativist or protectionist. Where Trump railed at Chinese exporters, British Leavers called for a bilateral free-trade deal with China. The only thing the two movements had in common was a sense of frustration with the Establishment.

That frustration stemmed, in both cases, from at least some shared causes. In both Britain and the United States, three factors in particular had contributed to a widespread disenchantment with the political class.

First, there was the Iraq War, and the subsequent belief that it had been launched on the basis of a deliberate lie. For what it's worth – and I write as one who opposed the invasion – I think George Bush and Tony Blair were mistaken rather than mendacious. After all, if they knew that there were no weapons of mass destruction in Iraq, they must also have known that the invading troops wouldn't find any. It would have been the stupidest lie in history. None the less, the episode served to widen the rift between politicians and people. A conviction began to take hold, including among respectable and educated voters, that their politicians were prepared to send young men off to die for some clandestine cause; a cause, at any rate, whose true purpose had not been fully adumbrated.

Second, there was the credit crunch, which saw hundreds of billions of pounds taken through the tax system from low- and medium-income families and given to . . . well, no one is entirely sure what happened to it. The crash that followed the collapse of Lehman saw middle-class families expropriated through the tax system in order to rescue some very wealthy bankers and bondholders from the consequences of their own errors. No wonder the politicians who decreed those bailouts were blamed. And no wonder faith in the system took a knock from which it has still not recovered.

Third, our age is witnessing a mass movement of populations, a *Völkerwanderung*, unknown in peacetime. Rising wealth and advances in technology have triggered a migration from the poorer parts of Asia, Africa and Latin America to developed nations.

I spent part of last summer volunteering in a hostel for underage migrants in the south of Italy. The boys staying there had come mainly from West Africa, and some had undertaken truly Odyssean journeys across first the Sahara and then the Mediterranean.

They were courageous, resourceful, optimistic lads, and the more time I spent with them, the more convinced I became that, in their position, I'd have done exactly as they had. Few of them, though, were refugees, at least not as that term is legally defined. They were fleeing poverty, misery and corruption, rather than war, oppression and persecution. And for each one who had come, a hundred were waiting to follow.

When we met people being landed by the Italian coastguard, their first question was often 'Where can I get Wi-Fi?' I don't mean to suggest that, because they had smartphones, they weren't in need. On the contrary, the phone was often their only possession of value. Smartphones are the key to the whole migratory phenomenon, making possible the transfers of credit and information that allow young people to move from Nigeria or Eritrea through Sicily or Greece into Northern Europe. To their grandparents, living on subsistence agriculture, such a trek would have been unthinkable.

People in the receiving countries are aware that these population movements are increasing. They keep hearing their leaders promising to do something about it, but nothing seems to check the flow. Some voters suspect that, for all their promises, the politicians don't really want to do anything about it. They wonder whether their elites secretly want more inward migration than they publicly admit, seeing it as a source of cheap nannies and gardeners rather than as a source of competitive pressure on jobs and amenities.

Put it all together and what do people see? A political class that will send boys to die in distant lands on the basis of, at best, a half-truth; that levies taxes on the poor to bail out the rich; and that supports an immigration policy designed for big business at the expense of ordinary people.

For what it's worth, I think only the second of these assertions is fair. But I can see why a gap has opened up between government and governed, between what the Italians call the *paese legale* and the *paese reale*, between (as a constituent of mine, a call-centre worker, put it) the smirking classes and the working classes.

The question is how to fill that gap. Will mainstream politicians offer a greater measure of democratic control? Can we aspire to make British voters as contented as, say, Swiss voters, who regularly tell pollsters that they are delighted with their system of regular referendums? Or will we leave the way open to some local version of Donald Trump or Beppe Grillo?

Dismissing the recent vote as essentially populist

or chauvinist risks causing a massive misdiagnosis and thus a faulty prescription. It is, perhaps, an understandable error, again deriving from behavioural psychology. It is natural to identify a cause with its most strident advocates. Think of how many English people say 'the Scots' when they really mean 'the SNP' – Scotland having very recently voted against independence. Or think of how many people, when they hear the word 'Muslims', think of long beards or burqas or even of Islamic terrorism, rather than of actual Muslim friends or workmates.

In much the same way, perhaps understandably, some observers, especially on the broadcast media, associate the Leave campaign with its angriest and loudest advocates. Hence their insistence, in defiance of the polling data, that the vote was 'all about immigration'. In my experience, if you're told that, you can be almost certain that you're talking to a Remain voter.

Britain, like all countries, has its share of bigots and racists. Some of them no doubt voted to quit the EU. But we know for a fact that most Leave voters want a measure of immigration from the EU to continue, and that 84 per cent of them want existing EU migrants to the UK to be allowed to stay.

If there was a populist tinge to the campaign, it was populism in its more exact sense: a reaction to oligarchic rule, a resentment of a ruling elite that seemed to be governing in its own, not the national, interest.

Speaking to a rally in Kent a week before the poll, I began to hymn that county's radical past, from the Peasants' Revolt to its support for the parliamentary cause in the civil war. When I mentioned the Peasants' Revolt, the audience interrupted with prolonged cheers. In their eyes, the EU referendum was partly about reminding the grandees and Euro-corporatists that they weren't the only people in Britain.

They had a point. Just as the original Peasants' Revolt was directed at an alien caste, a French-speaking aristocracy that maintained itself in power through a series of legal privileges, so the Leave campaign was aimed at various groups who had learned how to make a living out of Brussels.

The Remain campaign's very first move was to publish a letter in the *Independent* signed by the heads of various green pressure groups warning against Brexit on grounds that EU laws had 'a hugely positive effect' on the environment. It did not attempt to explain why a post-EU Britain wouldn't simply retain or replicate – or even improve – these 'hugely positive' laws. As so often, there was an insulting implication that voters needed to have such things handed down by their betters.

Most interesting, though, were the signatures at the end, representing Natural England, the Green Alliance, the Royal Society for the Protection of Birds, the Natural Environment Research Council and so on. Of the twelve organizations named, the European Commission funded eight directly – and others indirectly. But, of course, 'protect our countryside' sounds much prettier than 'protect our grants'.

Just as NGOs had learned how to parasitize the EU, so, more damagingly for the ordinary citizen, had large multi-nationals. The Remain campaign was funded by megabanks and corporate giants, including Goldman Sachs, J. P. Morgan and Morgan Stanley. Again, it's not hard to see why.

The green grandees' letter was followed by several more from Brussels-sponsored lobbies, including universities, charities and businesses. A letter in the (London) *Times* was signed by the bosses of thirty-six FTSE-100 companies. A moment's research showed that these companies had collectively spent €21.3 million lobbying the EU, and got back €120.9 million in grants from Brussels. It's hard to argue with a 600 per cent return on investment.

The money, though, is the least of it. Far more damaging is the way big firms lobby to get rules that suit them and hurt their competitors. I was surprised, when I was a new MEP, that corporate giants were forever demanding more regulation. It took me a while to understand why. They could easily assimilate the compliance costs, and were raising barriers to entry so as to secure a more monopolistic position.

The sums poured into lobbying rival anything seen in Washington – with the difference that, in Brussels, there is no countervailing pressure from the electorate. Here is a summary of what the big firms spent in the last six-month period for which figures are available:

Amount spent on lobbying in the first six months of 2015 (euros)

01 Microsoft Corporation	4,500,000
02 Shell Companies	4,500,000
03 ExxonMobil Petroleum & Chemical	4,500,000
04 Deutsche Bank AG	3,962,000
05 Dow Europe GmbH	3,750,000
06 Google	3,500,000
07 General Electric Company (GE)	3,250,000
08 Siemens AG	3,230,169
09 Huawei Technologies	3,000,000
10 BP	2,500,000

Source: Transparency International

There is nothing intrinsically wrong with lobbying. Personally, I have made it a rule not to deal with lobbyists as an MEP, but I'm aware that I'm being unfair to most of them. My complaint here is not about lobbying; it's about the way that the beneficiaries of lobbying were seeking to prejudice the democratic process, to secure a Remain vote that would serve their interests rather than that of the country as a whole. Is opposition to such a racket populist? If so, it's surely a justified populism: a legitimate reaction against an oligarchic tendency.

If you think 'oligarchy' is too strong a word, by the way, ponder this. An official working for the EU is exempt from national taxation, paying instead a token rate of European tax equivalent to around 21 per cent, flat.

Contemplate, for a moment, that extraordinary fact. The bureaucrats in the Commission and Parliament make decisions that have fiscal consequences for ordinary people, while themselves being exempt from those consequences. If that isn't oligarchy, what is?

When we consider the oddities of the French *ancien régime*, one of the greatest iniquities, to modern eyes, is that the aristocracy was largely exempt from taxation. We wonder at a system based on the legal and systematic expropriation by the rich of the poor. Yet we have re-created such a system in Brussels.

The tax exemption is only the most visible and flagrant example; in truth, the entire EU system is based around transferring wealth from ordinary citizens to those lucky enough to be part of the machine.

What we saw in the referendum was an overdue correction, a recovery of power from remote elites. We saw a vote of confidence in democracy itself, based on the conviction that the United Kingdom could flourish under its own laws, trading with friends and allies on every continent. Perhaps most dramatically, we saw the British people disregard the advice – no, the instructions – of those who presumed to be their betters. They ignored the hectoring, the bullying and the scare stories, and politely voted to recover the right to hire and fire their own lawmakers.

To explain why they were right – and to explain, perhaps, the outrage of some of the defeated – let me quote Burke again.

> Because half-a-dozen grasshoppers under a fern make the field ring with their importunate chink, whilst thousands of great cattle, reposed beneath the shadow of the British oak, chew the cud and are silent, pray do not imagine that those who make the noise are the only inhabitants of the field; that of course they are many in number; or that, after all, they are other than

the little shrivelled, meagre, hopping, though loud and troublesome insects of the hour.

Let's allow that there was a measure of anti-Establishment sentiment behind the Leave vote. You don't have to believe it was justified, though I happen to believe it largely was. The question is how to soothe that feeling.

Part of the answer lies in the field of economic policy, or more specifically monetary policy. Having just quoted the great Irish seer and father of conservatism, Edmund Burke, let me now turn to the political thinker who stands furthest from him along the political spectrum.

Karl Marx was wrong about pretty much everything. I don't just mean wrong in the broad moral sense – although, with a hundred million deaths carried out in his name, he has a good claim to be reckoned the greatest incitement to violence in human history. No, I mean wrong in the literal sense that every prediction he made failed to come true – except one.

Marx saw himself as a scientist rather than an ideologue. His followers treated his turgid writings not as a series of opinions, but as a catalogue of empirical truths. Yet his record as a forecaster could not have been worse.

Free markets, Marx wrote, would destroy the middle class, concentrating wealth in the hands of a tiny number of oligarchs. In fact, free markets have enlarged the middle class everywhere they have been allowed to exist.

The revolution, he wrote, would occur when the proletariat became sufficiently self-aware, something he expected to happen first in Britain and then in Germany. In fact, as the working classes in those countries became more educated, they shored up the established order; the revolutions happened (disastrously) in Russia, China and Cuba which, according to Marx, were conservative peasant societies.

Capitalism, he believed, was doomed: it would collapse under the weight of its own contradictions. In fact, when he wrote that in 1848, capitalism was already beginning to lift humanity to an unprecedented level of wealth – a process that has been accelerating ever since.

Marx's disciples are impervious to the failure of their prophet's doctrines. Like the religious casuists they despise, they fit events to their beliefs rather than the other way around. Those beliefs are surprisingly widespread.

Although you find few self-declared Marxists these days except in universities, many of his precepts have become mainstream. When we talk of 'exploitation' or 'wage slaves' or, come to that, 'capitalism', we are quoting the old cadger.

How many times have you heard it asserted that 'the rich are getting richer and the poor are getting poorer'? That idea, too, derives from Marx, who called his theory 'immiseration'. Until now, it has been as false as everything else he wrote: someone on benefits in a Western country today is better off than someone on average wages in 1930.

Yet, very recently, it has started to come true. When, in response to the credit crunch, central banks printed extra money, they pushed up the price of property. People who owned stocks, shares, houses and other valuable goods saw their wealth rise commensurately. People dependent on their wages fell behind.

After a century and a half of being solidly wrong, Karl Marx is being vindicated – by loose monetary policy. If we measure assets and debts, rather than income, the wealth gap has grown considerably. In Britain, the richest fifth of households are 64 per cent better off than they were a decade ago, while the poorest fifth are 43 per cent worse off. It's a similar picture in the United States and in most of Europe.

If you want an explanation for the rise of populism, look no further. Working-class voters in Western countries are reacting to something recent and, in peacetime, almost unprecedented: a real decline in wealth.

It is in our nature to be loss-averse. Innumerable studies by behavioural psychologists show the same thing: given the chance to win a large sum by staking a smaller one, we make the irrational decision to hold on to what we've got. Our pain when we drop a £20 note is far greater than our pleasure when we find one in the street. Behavioural psychologists also tell us that, faced with loss, we become frightened and angry, and vote accordingly.

The worst of it is that central banks show no sign of slowing. Mark Twain once wrote that, if all you have is a hammer, everything starts to look like a nail. In the minds of the US Federal Reserve, the Bank of England, the European Central Bank and the Bank of Japan, all they have is a printing press. Every new injection of cash lifts the markets, and the rush wears off more quickly each time.

Until now, the idea that the state should lose its monopoly over money has been seen as a fringe position held only by eccentrics like Ron Paul and Douglas Carswell. I have a feeling that that is about to change.

Having a hard currency, based on something independent of the state, such as a commodity or a blockchain, will eventually halt the transfer of wealth from wage-earners to *rentiers*. But there is a more immediate way to assuage public anxieties, to take the heat out of populism. Again, the answer lies in making decisions more local and more democratic.

I have already touched on the idea that councils should have greater control over taxation and spending, including more control over welfare. In the case of planning, I'd go further, devolving power to a yet more local level. I'd make more use of the referendum instrument, especially on local tax issues. But these reforms should not be seen simply as one-off transfers of power. We now have an opportunity, fundamentally, to rethink the unitary structure of the British state.

9

POWER TO THE PEOPLE

THROUGHOUT THIS BOOK, I have argued that
we must do more than simply leave the EU in the
technical sense of resuming our sovereignty. We should
use that process to address the concerns that pushed
people into voting Leave in the first place.

We need policies that will benefit lower-income
voters, notably by reducing the cost of living. We
need more devolution, democratization and decentralization. We need freer trade. We need to think like
a maritime rather than a continental nation. Instead
of ministers spending day after day at Brussels sum-
mits, we should renew our relationship with the rest
of the English-speaking world – that unique nexus of
language and law, custom and kinship, cherished

by diaspora communities in Britain and across the Commonwealth.

More than anything, the Leave vote was driven by a sense that the political class had become remote, self-serving and cut off from the general population. We won't address that concern if, after bringing power back from Brussels, we leave it curdling in Whitehall. We need to push power downwards and outwards, to local authorities or, better yet, to individual citizens.

Let's start with a hard fact about the referendum result. Two of the four component nations of the UK returned pro-EU majorities. Stating it that way can make the divergence sound starker than it really was: two in five people in Scotland and Northern Ireland voted Leave. None the less, the UK must work as a partnership of four. While, legally, the only majority that mattered was the UK-wide one, we should not push ahead as if (for this is how it would be perceived by Remainers in the two more northerly territories) the winning side may dictate terms to the losing side.

The chief declared motivation of Leave voters, by quite some margin, was a belief in democracy. Well then, let us respect democracy in its fullest sense. Let us take on board the concerns of the 48 per cent, including on free trade with the EU and on a continuing participation in the various joint programmes that we heard so much about during the campaign, such as Horizon 2020 (a scientific research fund) and Erasmus (a student exchange scheme). How valuable these programmes are is, in a sense, a secondary consideration. They account for a trivial proportion of the UK's budget contributions and, since the sectors concerned plainly feel strongly about them, we should continue to participate in the way that many non-EU states do, including Norway, Israel and Canada. Non-EU Switzerland, which has long collaborated with its European neighbours in scientific research, and hosts the CERN facility, is recognized by none other than the European Commission as the most innovative state in the world.

What of the specific concerns of Scottish and Northern Irish Remainers? Were they significantly different from those of Remainers in England and Wales? Not, at least as far as anyone has been able to discover, in Scotland, where those who voted to break away from the UK in 2014 were slightly more likely to vote Leave than their Unionist compatriots. Indeed, with every single SNP parliamentarian at Westminster and Holyrood backing the EU, that party was arguably more unrepresentative of its electorate than any other in Britain.

Before the vote, many observers, especially Scottish

Unionists, fretted that a discrepancy in the result would break up the United Kingdom. So far, there is absolutely no sign of it. Surveys taken since the referendum have suggested slight swings to Unionism in Scotland. As this book goes to press, the three most recent polls, by Survation, Kantar TNS and YouGov, all show opponents of independence ahead of where they were before the vote, with leads of 8 to 10 per cent.

The case for giving formalized weight to Scottish opinion is democratic rather than tactical. The Scottish administration should be involved in formulating the withdrawal platform, not as some manoeuvre to keep the Union together, but because that is the only fair-minded response to the differential referendum results.

The truth is that for now, there is no serious prospect of a second referendum in Scotland, for the same reason that there won't be a second EU referendum in the UK: voters would repeat themselves, with the added emphasis that people use when they weren't listened to the first time.

Attitudes may shift over time, of course: we can't know how Scots will feel in thirty years. But it already seems clear that Brexit has not boosted separatist sentiment, for the most obvious of reasons. As several SNP tacticians have been honest enough to admit since the vote, Brexit gives Unionists an additional argument that they didn't have in 2014. This time, Scotland wouldn't simply be voting for a different relationship with England; it would be voting to link itself to a secondary market (the EU) rather than its primary one (the rest of the UK). According to the Scottish government, Scotland's exports to the EU are worth £11.6 billion per year, compared to £15.2 billion for those to the rest of the world, and £48 billion to the rest of the UK.[45] Moreover, if Scotland applied to join the EU as a new member, it would be doing so without the UK rebate, and without the opt-out from accepting the euro.

If anything, independence from the EU should give the United Kingdom a renewed sense of national purpose. Scottish separatism and Euro-integrationism both began to gain widespread support in the 1970s as the UK went into decline. The early and mid-1970s were arguably our lowest moment as a nation: the era of the three-day week, prices and incomes policies, constant strikes, ballooning trade deficits, double-digit inflation and general gloom.

It was also a time when disdain for Britain, generally expressed as 'anti-colonialism', was a semi-official doctrine. Small wonder that some dreamed

45 *Moneyweek*, 17 September 2016

of being part of a European polity instead, while others groped back toward older patriotisms. Paul Johnson even argued in his history of Ireland that the resumption of violence in Ulster after half a century of relative tranquillity was a response to the growing sense, starting in the late 1960s, that Britain was on its way to being a failed state.[46]

What, after all, did Britishness mean any more? The United Kingdom had once self-defined as a country with moral purpose: a country that would wage war against slavery and tyranny, that would seek to spread free thinking, free trade and free institutions globally, that exalted the individual over the state when so many rival powers did the reverse.

That sense of national purpose waned when Britain came to think of itself as just another European country. With the exception of the Falklands War which was, so to speak, thrust upon it, it is hard to think of an occasion since the early 1970s when Britain pursued clearly defined national interests in a major foreign-policy initiative, as opposed to supporting wider Western or European interests. I have been constantly struck, as an MEP, by how many UK ambassadors in third countries act like members of

46 *Ireland: A Concise History from the Twelfth Century to the Present Day*, 1981

the Brussels diplomatic team, concentrating on, for example, urging their host states to join regional blocs that mimic the EU.

Outside the EU, Britain will be free to define a global vocation again: as a champion of the Commonwealth and Anglosphere, and as the leading global champion of free trade. When New Zealand, with a population one sixteenth of Britain's, began to use global trading structures to dismantle barriers, observers spoke of the 'New Zealandization of the WTO'. How much more might a G7 economy achieve if it were to open its markets? Free trade should not be seen as an economic proposition, but as a moral one: as a force for poverty alleviation, conflict resolution and social justice.

Might Nicola Sturgeon seek to use the disengagement talks as an opportunity to foster grievance in the hope of holding another independence referendum? Of course she might: she uses almost everything for that purpose, and there is no dishonour in a politician seeking to advance deeply held convictions by any means at hand. Still, it is hard to see what, specifically, she can ask for in the talks that will make separation likelier. Would she argue that Scotland should not take back control of agriculture or of fisheries, two fields of policy which would pass straight from Brussels to Edinburgh? Would she demand that uncontrolled immigration from the EU continue, something that Scottish voters oppose in precisely the same proportion as English voters? Or would she simply make demands that she knew to be impossible, hoping that her electorate would be too dim to see it – rarely a winning move for any politician?

Remember that most Scottish Remainers, like most English Remainers, now want the country to succeed. Don't make the mistake of thinking that the Twitter sociopaths hoping for economic catastrophe are in any sense representative of the mass of people who voted to stay in the EU. In the real world, as opposed to online, very few people are longing for a downturn so as to be able to say 'I told you so'. In the real world, as opposed to online, few Remainers despise people who voted differently, because they have friends and family who did so. In the real world, as opposed to online, many Remainers came to their decision only marginally, and never imagined that it gave them any sort of moral superiority.

Scottish anxieties about Brexit will be addressed in the same manner as English anxieties. They will ease as the project starts to work, as Britain becomes a freer economy, open to traffic and commerce from all over the world. Adam Smith's homeland will benefit hugely from new trade deals: India, for example, currently applies a swingeing 150 per cent tariff to imported whisky.

Scottish Remainers have the same broad concerns as English Remainers. But Northern Ireland, not for the first time, marches to a different drumbeat. There was, in the province, a palpable, if not a total, correlation between tribal identity and the way people voted.

I visited Northern Ireland three times during the referendum, campaigning in small towns and at county shows as well as in Belfast, and I detected a sectarian undertone that had almost faded away over the previous decade. (Being of Scottish Presbyterian background on one side and Ulster Catholic on the other, I perhaps have a keener nose for these things than most English people.) Audiences were self-segregating at debates, and you could generally guess which side someone was going to come down on before he had reached his point.

By the end, it had become a kind of local joke. The warm-up act before a Belfast TV debate I spoke in was a popular home-grown drag artist called May McFettridge (the alter ego of John Linehan). 'Which of youse is fer Leave?' she asked the audience. As the Leavers duly cheered, she muttered: 'Aye. Pradestants!'

I did meet a few Catholic Leavers and, in fairness, more than a few Protestant Remainers. Some of the dynamics visible in Great Britain applied in Northern Ireland, too, with regard to age, wealth and so on. Still, any return to confessional voting in Northern Ireland should worry us.

If I were to try to summarize the concerns of the Republican and Nationalist voters who backed Remain in a single sentence, it would be this: 'Why should we have our country partitioned again because of the way people in England voted?'

Since the Belfast Agreement, the issue of constitutional change has largely dropped off the political agenda. According to the last major survey before the vote, only 13 per cent of Northern Irish Catholics, and only 4 per cent of the total population, wanted immediate moves toward a united Ireland.[47] It is not hard to see why: the border has, in practical terms, disappeared. What real difference would a transfer of sovereignty make – other than saddling Northern Ireland with the debts that the Republic was forced by Brussels to take on during the banking crisis?

At the last two general elections in Northern Ireland, something approaching normal politics prevailed, with arguments about healthcare, grammar schools and the proposed John Lewis in Lisburn. Meanwhile, relations between London and Dublin are better –

47 *Belfast Telegraph*, 17 September 2013

far better – than at any time since 1921. Plainly, it is in no one's interest to return to a hard border and, with it, the possibility of renewed animosities.

Happily, there is no reason that the current arrangements should not continue when Britain leaves the EU (assuming that, at least for the moment, Ireland chooses to remain). The Common Travel Area has existed throughout the British Isles since 1923. It includes the UK and the Republic of Ireland, which are in the EU, as well as the Channel Islands and the Isle of Man, which are not. So we can say, as a matter of observable fact, that there is nothing to stop EU and non-EU states establishing a border-free zone among themselves.

No major party in London or in Dublin wants to bring back a land border. (In practice, travel documents are sometimes checked on sea crossings and on flights, which no one seems to mind.) So how, practically, can an external EU border be kept open?

Borders regulate the movement of two different things: people and goods. Let us consider them in turn.

A commonly voiced concern is that once Britain leaves the EU it will have to impose border checks in Ireland to stop a massive flow of EU nationals across the frontier. After all, the argument goes, a Pole could move perfectly legally from Gdansk to Dublin, then drive across to Newry and then move to Great Britain.

Well, yes he could. Alternatively, he could just fly directly from Gdansk to Luton or take the coach to Victoria. The fear about people crossing the land border into the UK is based on a misunderstanding of how our immigration policies work. It is stupendously unlikely that any EU national will require a visa to enter the UK: people may enter the UK visa-free from, among other places, Barbados, Georgia, Tunisia, Uruguay, Swaziland, Senegal and Kiribati. The issue of legality arises only if visitors seek to stay longer than the period covered by the visa-free arrangement, typically ninety days.

In other words, immigration control depends, not on turning people back at borders, but on knowing that they are in the country. Those who overstay are unable to work legally or apply for a National Insurance number and, if they are picked up by the authorities for any reason – a driving offence, say – they face deportation.

The only thing necessary to keep the current system in place is for Ireland and the UK to agree, as part of the Common Travel Area, to share all data on who has entered their territories. If a passport swiped at Rosslare or Shannon is logged in the same way as one swiped at Portsmouth or Stansted, then there is no need whatever to check documentation at the land border.

But what of goods? Here, the pressure for controls is likely to come from the Irish – or, rather, the EU – side. We can reasonably assume that outside the EU, the UK will have lower tariffs than now. So why wouldn't, say, an Australian exporter ship a consignment of wine to Belfast, have it driven across the border, and then reshipped from Cork to mainland Europe, thereby avoiding the EU's 32 per cent duty on New World wines?

As we saw in Chapter Four, this dilemma exists all over the world. There are many cases where countries A and B both have separate FTAs with country C, but not with each other. Arguably, the main function of the WTO is to lay down procedures for such situations, notably through rules of origin. In practice, there are very few areas where EU tariffs are high enough to justify the extra freight costs involved in an extra Belfast-to-Cork leg, let alone the risk of prosecution. Still, in theory, Britain could face a customs border.

Then again, customs checks are no longer nineteenth-century affairs, where officials in peaked caps and epaulettes inspect every bag at a border post. Goods are shipped by sea and by road, with an electronic trail showing their origin. The purpose of a customs post is to guard against fraud, not to inspect every passing vehicle.

If Britain were to agree a comprehensive free-trade

deal with the EU, it would find itself in a similar situation to, say, Switzerland. Lorries may be stopped on the Swiss frontier by officials on either side, their manifests may be checked and, if there is reason to be suspicious, their contents may be inspected. In general, though, there is an assumption that, since there are no tariffs between the EU and the Helvetic Confederation, goods can pass freely.

None the less, we must assume that the EU will want the capacity to check that what enters its territory from the UK has been declared. The Australian wine exporter in the example quoted above would not be able to move his product in bulk through a legitimate freight company. He would have to disguise it as something else, such as a product originating in Britain, and then move it surreptitiously.

The Republic could seek to check every consignment crossing from Northern Ireland but, in reality, this is simply not practicable. It couldn't police every road, let alone every vehicle. The border is criss-crossed by a latticework of lanes, many of them dating back to the public works projects designed to offer some income to local people during the monstrous famine of the 1840s. Even during the height of the Troubles in the 1970s, it was never possible to impose checkpoints across the entire frontier.

So Ireland, which has very clearly stated that it does not want a land border, would in any case find the imposition of such a border impractical. What, then, is the alternative? Surely it's obvious: to carry out any checks when goods are loaded in the Republic for transport by sea to the rest of the EU. Would this violate the integrity of the single market? Hardly. In many EU ports, goods from outside the Union sit alongside those from within. They are examined, verified and sorted all the time. Having checks at Dublin, Cork and other ports is the only practical way to carry out inspections, and makes land checkpoints redundant.

Just as there is no reason for Brexit to push Scotland toward separation, so there is no need for it to prejudice the warm and deepening friendship between the UK and Ireland. Instead, we should seek to use the process to deepen the various relationships within this archipelago while, at the same time, strengthening the sense of local democratic accountability.

Although there has been welcome progress toward devolution to large cities, the United Kingdom remains one of the most centralized states in the world. Within the EU, only Malta has weaker local councils – and Malta, frankly, is close to being a single extended conurbation. Three quarters of British local government finance comes from the Treasury, which often tells councillors what they must spend their budgets on.

Understandably, many people are put off standing for local office, or else give up after one term when they discover how hard it is to get anything changed. Turnout is commensurately low, and local elections are often treated as miniature referendums on the government of the day.

The feebleness of our local authorities often astonishes European observers, who think of Britain as a highly developed democracy. In most Continental countries, a successful career in local or regional government is seen as a prelude to national political office, and it is not unusual to find impressive mayors and assemblymen in their twenties and thirties controlling large budgets.

In *The Plan*, Douglas Carswell and I argued that there was no power exercised by Holyrood under the terms of the 1998 Scotland Act which could not, in England, be handled by our shires and cities. We urged a massive devolution of power to county and metropolitan councils, including control of welfare, transport and policing, and fiscal autonomy based on a local sales tax.

Since we wrote that book in 2008, things have moved on. Following the 2014 referendum, Scotland is gaining substantial new powers, not least in the field of taxation. This makes the case for some form of parallel devolution in England not just powerful but urgent.

The unilateral devolution of power to Scotland was always anomalous. As long ago as 1977, the anomaly was given a name by Enoch Powell. He named it after the constituency of the Scottish MP, Tam Dalyell, who had made it the basis of his objection to devolution: the 'West Lothian Question'. Simply stated, the West Lothian Question is as follows: 'Why should Scottish MPs at Westminster have a say over the internal affairs of England and Wales when they have no such say over the affairs of their own constituents?'

For example, the ban on hunting with dogs was pushed through in England with the votes of Scottish MPs, even though it did not apply in Scotland. In 2015, there was an attempt slightly to modify the legislation by allowing a pack of dogs to be used to flush out foxes for pest control. The SNP opposed the measure, even though it would have brought the law in England into line with the law in Scotland – an indication, perhaps, that, having failed to turn Scots against the Union, Nicola Sturgeon was seeking to turn English voters against it, or at least to convince them that the price was too high, as Parnell had done over the Union with Ireland in the nineteenth century.

The right to use more than two hounds to flush out a fox might be of tangential interest to most English voters, but the West Lothian distortion also meant that tuition fees and foundation hospitals were passed during the Blair years by Scottish MPs whose own constituencies were exempt.

None the less, the imbalance has so far been a greater problem in theory than in practice. Once Scotland becomes largely self-financing, the status quo will be unsustainable. It will simply not be tolerable to English people that their rates of taxation and spending should be set by Scottish MPs whose own voters would be unaffected.

The scheme set out in *The Plan* would be one logical answer to the West Lothian Question. Another would be some form of English Parliament, either composed of English MPs at Westminster and voting on certain days of the week, or else a wholly separate assembly meeting at Winchester or wherever. Yet another variant would be to make the House of Commons the English Parliament, coequal to the other three legislatures, and replace the House of Lords with a British assembly that would deal with UK-wide issues, such as defence and immigration.

Precisely what form a devolved or federal Britain might take is beyond the scope of this book. All sorts of questions would need to be addressed, from the way we select or elect an upper chamber to the question of representation for, or at least, a formalized input from, the Channel Islands, the Isle of Man and the Republic of Ireland. Although none of these territories will want to cede sovereignty, our day-to-day closeness, not only on economic matters, but on free movement, reciprocal welfare entitlements and the like, might merit something closer than bilateral ministerial meetings.

All these things should be up for discussion at a Constitutional Convention, which would examine how to adapt the British state in the light of our post-EU opportunities. It should look at the powers of local government, the role of the Upper House (whose present size and composition now surely render it indefensible) and the relationships within this archipelago. It should also consider ways to strengthen the various legislatures vis-à-vis their executives, and whether there is a greater role for direct democracy, including petition and referendum mechanisms.

Working wholeheartedly with the Scottish administration on a form of Home Rule that includes fiscal autonomy will, I hope, take the sting out of the differences over Brexit. Likewise, inviting the Republic of Ireland to participate should assuage the concern that leaving the EU means cold-shouldering our nearest neighbour.

To be clear, the case for a Constitutional Convention is not that we ought to pander to Scottish and Northern Irish Remain voters; it is something that ought to be done in its own right. Easier relationships within the British Isles will simply be, as it were, a happy bonus.

All these things – indeed, everything I have proposed throughout this book – are about restoring purpose and value to the ballot box, about bringing government closer to people.

Let me finish as I began by recalling why people voted Leave. The EU is not a fixed and stable structure; it is, as its leaders keep reminding us, constantly evolving, sucking in more powers to the centre. The question Britain faced on 23 June 2016 was not simply whether or not we liked the current EU, but whether we wanted to remain on that conveyor belt.

The failure of David Cameron's renegotiation put that question beyond doubt. Had he brought back any powers from Brussels, even trivial ones, he would at least have been able to claim a precedent. 'Look,' he might have said, 'this is still far from perfect, but at least we've shown that jurisdiction can flow back to the national capitals as well as to Brussels. In future, there are other things we'll be able to recover, too.'

In the event, the EU refused to make any concessions. Those who had wanted, as David Cameron kept putting it, 'for Britain to remain in a reformed EU' had their answer. There was no reformed EU. Or, rather, the reforms of the EU were going in the wrong direction. If Britain voted to Remain, it would be implicitly accepting those future agglomerations of power. Staying in would not mean staying put.

Since the British vote, the EU has made clear that it intends to continue with the project of amalgamation it began six decades ago. Jean-Claude Juncker has declared that 'Borders are the worst invention ever made by politicians'.[48] The French and German ministers have produced a joint statement as follows:

> Our countries share a common destiny and a common set of values that give rise to an even closer union between our citizens. We will therefore strive for a political union in Europe and invite the next Europeans to participate in this venture.[49]

As a first step toward realizing this vision, the twenty-seven remaining EU leaders have agreed to create a separate EU military structure – the very thing that Remain campaigners spent the referendum denying.

It was this destination that British voters rejected,

48 Speech at the Alpbach Media Academy, 22 August 2016
49 tvp.info 27 July 2016

not the notion of working with their immediate neighbours. Or, to put it differently, Britain could not remain only in the free market by voting to remain; the only way to decouple from the political union was to vote to leave.

I have no doubt that that decision will be vindicated as the EU, or at least the greater part of the EU, continues to coalesce. It is Britain that is now going with the current of history. Large regional blocs are a hangover from an earlier age, a vestigial survival from the era when clever people agreed that the gentleman in Whitehall – or, rather, Brussels – knew best.

That age has been made redundant by technology. As Robert Colvile shows in his study, *The Great Acceleration*, top-down government is unable to keep up with the pace set by an online generation. The gap between our dealings with the state and our interactions with almost anything else grows wider and wider. We now take it for granted that we can download music, lease a car or order our shopping with a couple of mouse-clicks. Compare that experience to, say, finding an NHS dentist or getting your child into the state school of your choice or applying to build an extension to your house.

Governments can respond by becoming more responsive, more local and more limited, shedding some of their functions altogether and contracting out others to more efficient actors. But we have seen beyond doubt that the EU is incapable of making such reforms. It is structured in such a way as always to seek more power, more centralization. The question is whether the UK can now go in the opposite direction.

We have many advantages: a high level of education and of internet penetration; a common-law system that comes up from below rather than down from above; a strong commitment to private property and free contract; an individualist culture.

The odd thing is that many of the people who, in a domestic context, favour localism and democratiz-ation, have tended to apply a wholly different set of principles when it comes to the EU. Think, for example, of the Liberal Democrats, who are now demanding a second referendum because they didn't care for the outcome of the first one – which, to remind you, they had originally demanded, but then voted against when the moment came.

Most of us, I suspect, have met Lib Dems who are subject to a curious Euro-doublethink. They want power decentralized at home, but are happy to see it centralized in Brussels. They oppose quangos, but are happy to be run by the greatest quango of all, namely the European Commission. They rail against unelected

peers and placemen, but not against unelected Eurocrats. They like referendums in theory, but dislike
them in practice.

Outside the relatively *dirigiste* EU, Britain has the
opportunity to become, in the pure sense of the word,
a more liberal society: pluralist, competitive and based
on the autonomy of the private citizen. If we focus on
devolution, we might win over at least some of those
who are currently irreconcilable Remainers. As with
Scottish and Irish Nationalists, this is not the reason
to decentralize the British state; it is, again, a bonus.

The best of it is that, by succeeding as an open
economy, we might finally encourage the EU, or at least
some members of it, into the reforms that they have so
far resisted. Perhaps our example might succeed where
our exhortations have failed.

Near the end of his short but brilliant life, Pitt
the Younger was honoured by a great banquet at the
Guildhall in 1805, at which he was hailed as the man
who had saved Europe from revolutionary France.
He replied: 'I return you many thanks for the honour
you have done me; but Europe is not to be saved by any
single man. England has saved herself by her exertions,
and will, as I trust, save Europe by her example.'

It is now in the interests of the EU as a whole for
Britain to leave amicably, open its markets and show

what a commercial nation can achieve. We must hope for, and work toward, prosperity in the Continent: wealthy neighbours make the best customers, and we all have a stake in each other's success. The problem until now has been that the homogenization of policy was holding everyone back.

Or, to flip it around, diversity, pluralism and experimentation work to everyone's benefit. Competition is not a hostile act, but the best way to raise standards across the board. Trade is not a means of domination, but the opposite – an eirenic, opulent and equalizing force.

Over the past nine chapters, I have suggested how to make Brexit advantageous for all sides. I have looked at how and when to trigger Article 50, so as to optimize our trading opportunities across the oceans as well as in Europe. I have considered how the process of securing better commercial arrangements might be expedited by joining existing trading associations, including NAFTA and EFTA – though not the EEA. I have argued that dismantling our tariff and non-tariff barriers might revitalize the entire world trading system, bringing great benefits to developing and agrarian economies, as well as to British consumers.

I have looked, too, at the way in which regulations are generated, and at how we can use Brexit to get away from the corporatist culture of Brussels. Trading on the basis of recognizing standards and qualifications and not imposing our own will transform our economy, giving domestic producers an incentive to lobby for deregulation, rather than raising barriers to entry. I have explored how to maximize the interests of our services sector, including our financial services, as they compete increasingly against non-EU rivals. I have touched on how the process can be used to soothe rather than antagonize separatists in Scotland and Northern Ireland and, in the process, revitalize local democracy in England and Wales.

I have examined our options on immigration. We need skilled workers, and we need them from the world beyond, not just from the EU. At the same time, we want to determine for ourselves roughly who comes in and roughly in what numbers. These goals are hardly incompatible, and it should be possible to secure them with the agreement of our European allies, possibly by drawing a distinction in law between the right to take up a particular job in the UK and the right to settle.

Not least, I have looked at how Brexit can bring about a general restructuring in Europe, allowing a core of politically united states to exist amicably within a wider European market to the advantage of all sides.

In truth, the negotiations need not be difficult, for

our goals ought to be complementary. All sides should want a phased and cordial process which allows the eurozone to deepen within a free-trade nexus of friendly states. The challenge has at least as much to do with tone as with substance.

My first speech to the European Parliament after the vote on 23 June was in French. It seemed polite in the circumstances, following Nigel Farage's 'You're not laughing now!' outburst. I explained that Britain had voted against the Brussels bureaucracy, not against our European allies. We wanted to keep the closest possible security, commercial and diplomatic links commensurate with living under our own laws. I finished: '*Vous allez perdre un mauvais locataire. Vous allez gagner un bon voisin*' – 'You will lose a bad tenant and gain a good neighbour.'

Which brings me to the final and wholly unlooked-for bonus of independence: it will, if well handled, lead to better relations between Britain and its European allies. Think of all the quarrels we have had with our partners over the past forty years. Almost all of them have been about the same thing, namely the cost and nature of European integration. Tap that stone from our shoe and things ought to become easier and more comfortable for all sides. Brexit is now the greatest gift we can give our neighbours.

ARTICLE 50 OF THE TREATY ON EUROPEAN UNION

1. Any Member State may decide to withdraw from the Union in accordance with its own constitutional requirements.

2. A Member State which decides to withdraw shall notify the European Council of its intention. In the light of the guidelines provided by the European Council, the Union shall negotiate and conclude an agreement with that State, setting out the arrangements for its withdrawal, taking account of the framework for its future relationship with the Union. That agreement shall be negotiated in accordance with Article 218(3) of the Treaty on the Functioning of the European Union. It shall be

concluded on behalf of the Union by the Council, acting by a qualified majority, after obtaining the consent of the European Parliament.

3. The Treaties shall cease to apply to the State in question from the date of entry into force of the withdrawal agreement or, failing that, two years after the notification referred to in paragraph 2, unless the European Council, in agreement with the Member State concerned, unanimously decides to extend this period.

4. For the purposes of paragraphs 2 and 3, the member of the European Council or of the Council representing the withdrawing Member State shall not participate in the discussions of the European Council or Council or in decisions concerning it.

   A qualified majority shall be defined in accordance with Article 238(3)(b) of the Treaty on the Functioning of the European Union.

5. If a State which has withdrawn from the Union asks to rejoin, its request shall be subject to the procedure referred to in Article 49.

ABBREVIATIONS AND ACRONYMS

ALDE	Alliance of Liberals and Democrats for Europe
AMR	Advanced Market Research
ASEAN	Association of Southeast Asian Nations
BSE	Britain Stronger in Europe
CAP	Common Agricultural Policy
CBI	Confederation of British Industry
COMECE	Commission of Bishops' Conference of the European Community
ECB	European Central Bank
ECJ	European Court of Justice
EEA	European Economic Area
EEC	European Economic Community
EFTA	European Free Trade Association
EPP	European People's Party
EU	European Union
FCO	Foreign & Commonwealth Office
FTA	free trade agreement
GCC	Gulf Cooperation Council
GDP	gross domestic product

HMRC	Her Majesty's Revenue & Customs
IFS	Institute for Fiscal Studies
IMF	International Monetary Fund
MEP	Member of the European Parliament
Mercosur	Mercado Común del Sur (Common Market of the South)
NAFTA	North American Free Trade Agreement
NATO	North Atlantic Treaty Organization
NGO	non-governmental organization
NSPCC	National Society for the Prevention of Cruelty to Children
OBR	Office for Budgetary Responsibility
OECD	Organisation for Economic Co-operation and Development
OEEC	Organisation for European Economic Co-operation
ONS	Office for National Statistics
OPEC	Organization of the Petroleum Exporting Countries
PAYE	Pay As You Earn
REACH	Registration, Evaluation, Authorization and Restriction of Chemicals
RSPB	Royal Society for the Protection of Birds
SDLP	Social Democratic and Labour Party
TDI	turbocharged direct injection
TTIP	Transatlantic Trade and Investment Partnership
UNED	Universidad Nacional de Educación a Distancia (National University of Distance Education)
VAT	value-added tax
WWF	World Wide Fund for Nature
WTO	World Trade Organization